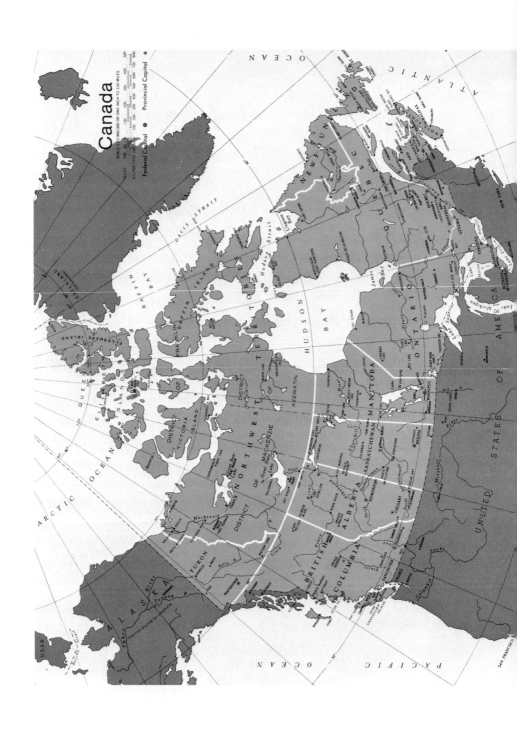

Canada

Canadian-American Relations

The Promise and the Challenge

Kenneth M. Curtis

John E. Carroll
University of New Hampshire

LexingtonBooks
D.C. Heath and Company
Lexington, Massachusetts
Toronto

Library of Congress Cataloging in Publication Data

Curtis, Kenneth M., 1931–
   Canadian-American Relations

   Bibliography
   Includes index.
   1. United States—Relations—Canada.   2. Canada—Relations—United
States.   I. Carroll, John E. (John Edward), 1944–   .   II. Title.
E183.8.C2C89 1983   327.73071   83–47990
ISBN 0-669-06793-8

45,900

Copyright © 1983 by D.C. Heath and Company

Third printing, September 1984

Published simultaneously in Canada

Printed in the United States of America on acid-free paper

International Standard Book Number: 0-669-06793-8

Library of Congress Catalog Card Number: 83-47990

*To the hope that all North Americans will
come to realize the benefit of healthy
Canadian-American relations.*

Contents

Foreword

No American concerned with public affairs can afford to ignore the importance of relations with Canada. Beyond the ever-present fact that our two nations share a continent—and all that entails—our societies are linked in many ways. Economically, we are each other's largest trading partners, a fact often overlooked in discussions of international economic issues. Militarily, we shoulder the responsibility of defending the vast continent of North America. Culturally and politically, we share the diverse ethnic heritages brought to this continent by generations of immigrants, and benefit from the democratic freedoms they cherished. There is no other country with which the United States has more in common.

Despite the importance of our relations with Canada, however, Americans have often taken Canada for granted. Perhaps because our relations have been strong for a long time, we believe that they will always remain so. Perhaps because we are preoccupied with urgent issues elsewhere, we believe there is less need to concern ourselves with the problems close to home that seem less pressing. Whatever the cause, the tendency to take Canada for granted is a grave mistake.

In the recent past, several difficult issues have troubled our mutual relations. Canada's recognition of Cuba and differences with U.S. policy in Latin America, most notably with U.S. policies toward El Salvador, are recent examples. The extensive economic interdependence of the United States and Canada has fueled new problems as groups in each country seek to contain the effects of worldwide economic difficulties. Protectionist pressures have arisen in many countries, but they have assumed an added dimension in the United States and Canada because of the magnitude of our trading relationship. In addition, recent Canadian efforts to control direct American investment have raised serious and legitimate concerns for parties on both sides of the border. These concerns must at least be addressed, if not resolved, in a complete and cooperative manner if strong ties between the two countries are to be sustained.

Other troubling questions concern the protection of the environment and use of energy. While environmentalist issues have long posed questions about the two countries' use of the Great Lakes, new and potentially more-difficult problems have recently emerged. Acid rain which drifts across our mutual border is now a major topic in bilateral relations. Other disagreements have concerned the routes that oil tankers travel as they bring fuel to the United States, and access to and use of Canadian energy resources.

Anyone who would dismiss these questions as unimportant would do well to look at the history of relations between our two countries. These relations began amid suspicion, as Americans broke dramatically with the British Crown, and Canadians chose an alternate path. Although there has been no military conflict between Americans and Canadians since the War of 1812, tensions between the two neighbors continued throughout the 1800s, fueled by the fear that American expansion might move north, as well as west.

Strong, friendly relations between the United States and Canada were actually forged only in this century. Since then, we have worked together diligently to cement strong ties, fought together as allies in two world wars, and cooperated in vast projects such as the construction of the St. Lawrence Seaway. Both our societies have now reached standards of living emulated by much of the rest of the world. Indeed, the governments of the United States and Canada have become models not only in their relations with their own citizens, but in their ties with each other. There are no two countries which share a longer border so peaceably and cooperatively.

This bilateral climate must, nonetheless, continue to be nourished if it is to be sustained. This book is thus both timely and important. It is written by two authors with a wealth of knowledge and practical experience relating to American-Canadian diplomacy, who shed new insight on the importance of continued healthy relations.

Kenneth Curtis, a man whom I admire immensely, served from 1967 to 1975 as the governor of Maine, a state which shares two-thirds of its land border with Canada. As governor, Mr. Curtis created many innovative programs in direct cooperation with Canadian provinces. Under his leadership Maine became the first state to establish an Office of Canadian Relations to coordinate this activity. From 1979 to 1981, Mr. Curtis served with great distinction as our ambassador to Canada.

Dr. John Carroll, associate professor of environmental conservation at the University of New Hampshire, is an expert in energy and international environmental and natural-resource relations. Dr. Carroll has written extensively on environmental diplomacy, acid rain, and many of the other U.S.-Canadian border problems. He has also acted as advisor to Governor Hugh Gallen of New Hampshire on U.S.-Canadian energy relations, and was appointed by Governor Richard Snelling of Vermont as United States representative to the Northeast International Committee on Energy (U.S.-Canada) in 1979. He thus brings to this volume a very important expertise in some of the most critical issues facing our two countries.

In their book, Curtis and Carroll provide a thorough and perceptive description of the important problems and issues confronting American-Canadian relations, explaining both the situation today and its ramifications for the future. They analyze and recommend not only how governmental policies should be altered, but how present institutions can be strengthened to ensure better communication and discussion of bilateral issues. Their recommendations are thoughtful and should be given serious consideration by Americans and Canadians alike. Their work constitutes an important contribution to discussion of American-Canadian relations, and will be valuable to anyone seeking a greater understanding of this important subject.

Cyrus R. Vance

Preface

A televised glimpse of the Great Wall of China some years ago captured the imagination of the U.S. people like the discovery of a new land, and sent businessmen scrambling for a piece of newfound opportunity. We applauded the historic normalization of relations with China. But what if there existed a country second only to the Soviet Union in area and capable of providing two-way trade with the United States more than twice that of any other country, and as well contribute more than one-fifth of all of our foreign trade? What if that country were rich in energy resources, shared many of our values, and had been located right next door all along?

It may sound absurd to suggest that many living in the United States might not understand the breadth and the depth of Canadian-U.S. interdependence. Yet many Americans view Canada, their northern neighbor, as either a small nation full of friendly people or the fifty-first state. U.S. foreign relations with Canada have often been conducted with a similar lack of sensitivity and appreciation for the magnitude of that relationship.

We do not wish to suggest that Canada receives no benefit from the accident of its geographic location. Nor do we intend to create a balance sheet of benefits or advantages of the U.S.-Canadian relationship. It is, however, our hope to contribute to a wider understanding of the critical nature of that relationship, and its rich promise for the future; to bring an awareness and appreciation of the uniqueness of this relationship to the people of both countries; to examine present-day problems and failures; and to describe the way that promise is now being threatened.

Canadian-
American
Relations

1 A Future of Harmony or Disharmony

It is well to acknowledge that . . . there can be no pretense of describing in a full-bodied way the scope and the intricacy of this relationship. We are dealing with an ongoing interplay of vastness and intimacy—of similarities and differences, of the past and the present, of the public and the private—all gathered together in a drama of disparities and of alternating attraction and rejection that has no counterpart in the international community. In such an interplay where there is room for almost anything to be both true and untrue, the overall portrayal must be a considered judgement.[1]

With these words John Sloan Dickey, Canadian-American scholar and distinguished president of Dartmouth College, began his instruction of his fellow Americans on what he referred to as the "American presence" in North America and Canada's response to that presence. He then summarized the implications of this presence for Canada's past and future. He also discussed the repercussions to Americans from the Canadian reaction to the U.S. geographical, economic, and to some extent, political dominance over its people and nation.

Today, a decade after these words were written, at a time of serious problems in the bilateral relationship, problems that are perhaps unsurpassed in living memory, it is time for Americans to take another look at the effects of this U.S. continental presence and conduct toward Canada. It is time for them to ask if the North American status quo is as it ought or must be; to ask themselves if they wish to accept the costs of continuing on the divergent course that began a decade ago or if they are willing to choose harmony over disharmony by displaying understanding or, at the least, a willingness to make short-term sacrifices for the long-term good.

The U.S.-Canadian relationship is inherently a close one for a number of reasons, including the sharing of common values between the two peoples, the existence of a high level of economic interdependency, and the important positions both nations have historically given to human rights. Writings on the relationship more often concentrate on the differences, however, and these too are real and must be given due consideration. The basis of conflict between the nations is the dominant position of the United States due to its much greater population (a ten-to-one ratio), the size and dominance of its markets over Canada's, and its world-power status. U.S. control in these as well as in cultural areas often engenders in Canadians a conscious sensitivity and, understandably, a defensive posture described in Professor Dickey's book as the underlying root of Canadian nationalism.

1

As the larger of the two nations, the United States perhaps feels little urgency to pay attention to its northern neighbor. After all, from a traditional diplomatic viewpoint Canada is assumed to be totally in the sphere of U.S. influence. Furthermore, on the level of human relations most of the Americans who visit or form impressions of Canada take this seemingly very similar nation of twenty-four million people for granted. And yet, the question arises whether the United States can afford to make these assumptions about the world-scale "middle power" on its doorstep that is its best customer and best supplier of raw materials. Is it wise to take for granted any nation as advanced or as sophisticated as Canada, a nation with a standard of living only slightly lower than that of the United States?

Due in part to this overshadowing by the United States, Canada has often been described as a nation in search of an identity. While this analysis was quite correct ten years ago, on the rapidly changing domestic scene in Canada a feeling of independence and global importance is growing. One reason for this change is that by repatriating the British North America Act from England (that is, bringing home constitutional amending authorities) Canada now has its own constitution, which is in itself symbolic of independence. Other reasons for this growing feeling of independence exist, however, that are perhaps more substantive.

Canada is enormous, second in size only to the Soviet Union, and a vast repository of natural resource wealth in minerals, in timber, in food, in energy, and, perhaps most importantly, in skilled manpower and sophisticated scientific technology and capability. This insures its place as one of the world's most-important middle powers. On the world market the country serves as a major supplier of such basic raw material commodities as wood pulp, lumber, coal, wheat, copper ores and concentrates, and nickel ores and concentrates. Canada is also a major source of automotive vehicles, engines and parts, newsprint, copper- and nickel-finished products, and various types of machinery (such as farm, construction, and drilling).

Canada is one of the world's leading mineral producers, ranking as the world's largest producer of asbestos, nickel, zinc, and silver. It is second in the production of potash, molybdenum, gypsum, uranium, and sulfur, and among the world leaders in the production of titanium concentrates, platinum, gold, copper and iron ore. This array of mineral resource wealth coupled with a low population makes the country highly dependent on export sales in the world market.

Canada's vast forests are equally if not even more significant than its mineral wealth; it may in fact be the nation most dependent on forest resources, forest industry, and forest exports. Forests are the source of at least one-fifth of Canada's total exports, and almost half of all the newspaper pages printed in the non-Communist world are printed on Canadian newsprint.

Canada also maintains world-scale fishery and agricultural production. A well-established government-subsidized fishing fleet on both Atlantic and Pacific coasts and a proven ability to grow wheat and other crops on a world scale make Canada a food-producer of some significance. Both of these industries are substantially based on export.

Finally, vast amounts of coal and natural gas, coupled with significant reserves of oil and uranium and some of the world's leading developed and potentially developable hydropower production sources, place Canada in the position of a major energy producer. The export of hydroelectricity is restricted for geographical reasons to the United States; but the other reserves, particularly coal and natural gas (as well as many areas of energy technology), are available to an obviously hungry world market.

For these and other reasons, Canada is a land worth knowing. And yet, Americans in general know surprisingly little and understand less of this nation and its people. What they do know is often wrapped in misconceptions or myth. Notwithstanding the signficant efforts of the Canadian government outreach programs, conducted through its embassy and consulates over the past few decades, Americans still know very little fact and have even less insight into this highly sophisticated and globally conscious society north of the border. While some isolationists might argue that ignorance is bliss, this state of affairs is undesirable and insulting at best, costly or even dangerous at worst. It is in the national interests of both peoples that the American people develop a greater and more insightful knowledge of their fellow North Americans. The authors hope that this book will contribute in at least a small way to that goal.

As previously mentioned, the increasingly serious problems in U.S.-Canadian relations appear to be of far greater magnitude than the cyclical periods of tension our extensive relationship has heretofore produced. The authors of this book perceive the bilateral relationship as in a state of deterioration, with a resulting harm to the interests of both peoples if such deterioration is allowed to continue. Possibilities for improved interaction lie in the increasing opportunities for joint collaboration on major and minor projects as well as in the opportunity for joint problem solving. At the same time, among the greatest costs of the deteriorating relationship could be the loss of these opportunities and a souring of the climate under which such collaboration can be initiated.

If this happened, North Americans in the broadest sense would be the losers, as would be those nations who look to the United States and Canada for leadership in human rights, democratic ideals, and—of growing importance—the supply of food and assistance to those in need. Canadian-American amity has global significance, both in terms of stability and peace and also in terms of what these two nations can accomplish in their joint compassion for the deprived peoples of the developing world. Canada's special links to French-speaking Africa and Asia and its Commonwealth ties to the former British Empire can well be coupled with the vastness of American means and technology to forge a leadership role for the two countries in the North-South dialogue, and the new world order that may well be its aftermath. Because of their differences in population size and place in the world, Canada and the United States can readily complement each other, thereby accomplishing ends in the long-range best interests of both.

A stronger and more independent Canada can help both nations immeasurably, as well as much of the rest of the world, especially if they work in tandem, and the United States will be a much stronger nation in the long term. John Sloan Dickey introduced this concept. We affirm and build upon it.

Note

1. John S. Dickey, *Canada and the American Presence: The United States Interest in an Independent Canada* (New York: New York University Press, 1975), p. vii. Reprinted with permission.

2

The Politics and Diplomacy of Bilateral Relations

From the Beginning to the Present

That long [Canadian] frontier from the Atlantic to the Pacific Oceans, guarded only by neighborly respect and honorable obligations, is an example to every country and a pattern for the future of the world.[1]

With these words, Sir Winston Churchill offered the ultimate compliment to the friendship and trust of two peoples.

The "longest unguarded frontier" (5,335 miles including Alaska) is perceived by many Canadians as an overused cliche, a phrase used by those who know little else about their country. Actually, Canada once did have a need to defend its border against the very real threat of military invasion—invasion from none other than the colonial Americans. U.S.-Canadian relations were born in war and bloodshed in an era when Americans chose violent rejection of the status quo and revolted against the established authority of the Crown, while Canadians chose a slower, more peaceful devolution from overseas authority. This difference in philosophy, coupled with the American invasion of Canada to capture Montreal and the constant threat of invasion elsewhere, began the bilateral relationship on a military note. These early differences were reinforced by the migration of many loyalists to the Crown who left the American colonies under duress, migrated to the Maritimes, parts of Quebec, and eastern Ontario, and demanded protection. With the decisive climax of the American Revolution, the delimitation of the border itself was begun.

The nervous years of the late eighteenth and early nineteenth centuries culminated in a further U.S. threat to Canada embodied in the conflict Americans call the War of 1812. In this bloody war extensive action took place on the lower Great Lakes. Once again, U.S. forces invaded Canadian territory (Ontario, then known as Upper Canada) and were rebuffed. Through the settlement of this conflict came the solidification of long portions of the border.

The postwar period from 1815 to the 1850s was one of "manifest destiny," of national expansion for Americans, an era that saw tremendous expansion of the United States. Vivid memories of the earlier wars and the increasing evidence of an American desire to expand its borders further caused the relatively small population of Canadians strung out across the

5

U.S. northern border to fear annexation. Watching the United States deal with Mexico and the British interests in the far Northwest fed these fears.

The pre-Civil War period, and then the war itself, distracted American interest from national expansion. The threat to Canada did not end, however; it just took on another form. Initial fear of a spillover of this bloody conflict into Canada was replaced by a concern that the heavily armed and victorious Union Army, fired by the rhetoric of some politicians, could conceivably become threatening.

The remainder of the century was colored by the resurrection of U.S. policy based on the theory of manifest destiny. Canadian fears were reinforced by the purchase of Alaska, the rapid settlement of the West, and successful U.S. boundary negotiations with Great Britain (wherein, in the eyes of many Canadians, the Americans and British carved up Canada against the interests of a still not fully independent Canada. As in the earlier years of the century, annexation rhetoric from American politicians, not the least of whom was President Theodore Roosevelt, kept the U.S.-Canadian relationships tense. Only when the eyes of both peoples were forced to turn globally did this long era of war, mistrust, and general nervousness over bilateral relations on the Canadian side finally come to an end.

The era of modern-day collaboration and friendship began with the necessities of North American involvement in the first great global conflict. For Canadians this was a long and very costly four-year commitment (1914–1918), while for Americans it was shorter and less costly in many ways. Canada's many war monuments include memorials to the dead for wars in which the United States was not involved, such as the Boer War and the Crimean War. More significantly, they include memorials that denote extensive and costly involvement in the two world wars—1914–1918 and 1939–1945—in which the isolationist and reluctant United States finally, to the Canadian mind, accepted its responsibilities. However, the dynamics of an unstable world ultimately forced collaboration in both world wars; and the empathy that resulted from surviving a long economic depression together in the intervening years clearly ended many of the earlier differences. These experiences demonstrated to both peoples, for the first time, the value and necessity of joint collaboration.

The period between the wars was also characterized by the end of British dominance over the Canadian economy and the replacement, in many respects, of Britain's economic position by that of the United States. Following the cessation of military activity in the 1940s, this transferal of roles led directly to an era of joint collaboration on larger-scale "megaprojects" designed to enhance the well-being of both peoples. From the ambitious St. Lawrence Seaway and Niagara Falls hydropower developments, the Welland Canal, the North American Air Defense Command (NORAD), greater management of the Great Lakes, and negotiation of the Auto Pact to the

Columbia Treaty of the early 1960s, the U.S.-Canadian relationship in this era must be classified as one of the closest in their history. Much of great substance was achieved and many unique diplomatic initiatives and accomplishments were made.

Some commentators would also say, however, that in this era, a period that led to an inevitably higher level of economic integration, were sown many of the seeds of present-day bilateral problems. This economic integration has meant a higher material living standard for Canada but has not occurred without costs. For example, some Canadians are not happy with the high concentration of U.S.-based corporations in Canada or the concept of "draining Canadian resources" to serve the insatiable U.S. appetite for energy and raw materials. The tradeoff for material benefits has been in the form of Canada's partial sacrifice of independence and power. Still, the world, and probably most Americans, have formed an image of positive U.S.-Canadian relations from the great works and accomplishments of this era.

From the wellsprings of this postwar integration and its attendant costs has sprung increased Canadian nationalism. At the same time, many U.S. policies, and actions, have escalated this nationalism into pockets of anti-Americanism. Modern-day examples of divergence between these two nations are not difficult to find. The strong reaction of many Canadians against significant elements of U.S. foreign policy, initially against American involvement in Vietnam and, more recently, against the nature of U.S. involvement in a variety of underdeveloped nations (including El Salvador, where there is Canadian sympathy for the side opposed by the United States) are leading to new political directions separate from those of the United States.

In 1972 the Nixon administration, breaking with tradition by failing to exempt Canada from strongly protectionist U.S. trade policy at considerable disruption to the Canadian economy, signaled to many observers the end of the special relationship between the two nations. Recent rhetoric over Canada's Foreign Investment Review Act shows a continuing divergence in economic policy. The U.S. Senate's failure to ratify the East Coast Fisheries Treaties as negotiated (see chapter 4), current imbalance in the Auto Pact (which substantially favors the United States) (see chapter 3), and the Reagan administration's strong stance against Canada's National Energy Program, whereby the Canadian government seeks to reduce the 70 percent U.S. multi-national ownership and control of Canada's oil and gas industry, have further reinforced Canada's drive to set new economic directions away from its continental partner and toward the rest of the world.

The most recent U.S. recession, characterized by high interest rates, high unemployment, and decline in the GNP, has had serious economic repercussions in Canada. It has been said of the countries' economic relationship that when the United States sneezes, Canada catches pneumonia. Not only does the Canadian economy respond to even minor changes in U.S. policy or economic conditions; but when the United States suffers, Canada, being deprived of the resilience of the U.S. economy, suffers even more. Rising at this time as well are the voices for protectionism that evolve naturally during such periods of economic difficulty. These voices are often a threat to the bilateral relationship because of the high level of trade interdependence involved in that relationship.

As the 1980s have unfolded, Canada has shown an increasing desire to separate its destiny from that of the United States, a turnabout that could not only erase much of the progress toward common goals achieved in the twentieth century but also hasten the loss of these opportunities to work together—opportunities so badly needed by both countries as well as by the world. A further potential result is a return to the mistrust and anxiety so prevalent in the preceding century.

A Public and Private Relationship

The U.S.-Canadian public relationship, like any other relationship between nations, has its formal diplomatic side; hence it has its share of country desks, embassies, consulates, diplomats, and the protocol and formality of international diplomacy. All similarity with relationships with other nations ends there, however. If the United States were to clearly define its foreign policy with respect to Canada, it would be built upon a bilateral relationship unique among the nations of the world.

That relationship is in a sense a private relationship, an informal arrangement involving a steady flow of goods, people, and communications across the border. This flow is almost incalculable in extent and involves people from every walk of life and every geographical region of both nations; and it proceeds, overwhelming any attempt at diplomatic control, largely outside of—indeed in spite of—the diplomatic relationship. Labor unions, doctors, researchers, educators, and environmentalists are some of the groups regularly involved in conferences where new ideas and developments can be shared. A steady, easy relationship has evolved, one of blood and family ties, of close friendship, of intimate business and professional relationships, all of which ignore the border and sometimes even deny its reality.

Between the formal and private involvements is found a third dimension of interaction that plays a major role in shaping the relationship. Both countries are characterized by vast distances and regional differences of interests; thus a natural north-south dialogue has evolved that is based on regional, not national boundaries. For example, the New England governors and Eastern Canadian premiers meet annually to discuss wide-ranging subjects for cooperative action; and more recently, the western governors have been inviting the Western Canadian premiers to their meetings. A number of other illustrations can be found in chapter 7, which deals with state-provincial relations.

Bilateral governmental involvement occurs on various levels. Congress has now become separately involved in the Canada-U.S. Interparliamentary Group, which meets on a regular basis to discuss bilateral concerns. Canadian ministers meet frequently with their counterparts in the president's Cabinet to discuss and negotiate issues within their spheres of responsibility. Government officials are involved in a steady flow of meetings and daily direct-dialed telephone communications.

Indicative of the relative importance of the United States to Canada, the Canadian Department of External Affairs devotes an entire bureau, a major sub-division, to diplomatic relations with the United States, backed by the strong support of a number of major departments of the federal bureaucracy. Canada's largest (and probably most important) embassy is in Washington, invariably headed by an ambassador of prominence in the Canadian foreign service. It is staffed from among the best of Canadian diplomats and is supported in the field by fourteen large consulates-general (impressive by U.S. standards) in major American cities. The Canadian consular staffs are large, highly professional, and active travelers in their assigned regions. While representing their country to the American people, they gather information and, more importantly, insight of importance to Ottawa's interests. (Given the amount of attention that Canada gives to the United States, Canadian government officials sometimes feel rebuffed and at times insulted by the lack of a similar response.)

Symptomatic of the relatively unimportant position Canada commands in Washington, however, the United States too often fails to consult Canada before setting forth foreign policy initiatives of interest to the Western Alliance. It is not unusual for a State Department official to be dispatched to inform Canada and ask for its cooperation on a policy hours after it has been announced through a media that reaches Canadian people at the same time it reaches U.S. citizens. Partly due to the disparity in the size of our governments, it is also not unusual for a Canadian minister to be dealing not with his or her counterpart but with someone at a lower level. If the issue involved is a major or public one in Canada, this type of insensitivity makes the Canadian minister appear weak to his constituents and the United States appear uncaring.

Indicative of a nation that considers Canada to be within its sphere of influence and perhaps thereby requiring less attention, the U.S. diplomatic effort in Canada is minimal. It is characterized by a very small Office of Canadian Affairs at the Department of State, a small embassy in Ottawa, and six scattered consulates that are small in size, severely overburdened, and underbudgeted.

At the State Department in Washington, Canadian issues are dealt with through the Division of Europe and Canada, which is directed by an assistant secretary of state. This minimal commitment—though the means of providing a surprising amount of information and service to its government—does not demonstrate the influence and support required for a badly needed overview of the bilateral relationship as a whole. Unlike that with any other nation, the U.S. interaction with Canada tends to be managed in an ad hoc dispersed manner. When a problem arises, it is often handled by the federal agency involved, which frequently proceeds to negotiate and be the U.S. spokesman in its narrow sphere of interest without consideration for any overall policy toward Canada. Inconsistency and sometimes contradiction have come to mark U.S. behavior.

One is left with the clear impression that the United States has judged any of a number of smaller, more distant countries to be worthy of more diplomatic attention than Canada. Americans, even while maintaining strong personal ties and a unique form of interaction with Canada, tend to take their northern neighbor for granted. Such an approach is justified by the fallacious argument that it is not necessary for the United States to devote attention to nations already within its sphere of influence. Conversely, the private or nongovernmental interaction is very strong, as will be seen in later chapters.

What is surprising, however, is that the United States devotes such little attention to a major nation at its doorstep, which is in fact, its number one supplier of imports and its number one market for exports. This disparity in diplomatic effort appears to be a reflection of the two societies as a whole. It ignores the reality, however, that Canada and the well-being of Canada is critical to the future of the United States.

Three Issues: Environment, Defense, and International Affairs

It is our premise that these two North American peoples profit from each other, lead better lives because of each other, and, in essence, *need* each other. Of all the many aspects of this continental interdependency, this book focuses on three areas that do not receive sufficient attention. The first is internal and relates to the sharing of the continental commons. The second is external and relates to survival in a troubled and unstable world. The third concerns the opportunity and the benefits that could accrue through relations with other nations.

Americans, who are ten times more numerous than their Canadian counterparts, sometimes need reminding that they are situated in North

America with a large neighbor, whether they like it or not. Just as Canadians must often adjust to the reality of American "bigness," so must Americans come to adjust to Canadian "bigness" in another sense. They share a substantial continental commons: common marine and inland waters and all species that inhabit them; common air masses; and perhaps even a common stake in the Arctic (because of not only the geographical position of Alaska and Canada but also common defense and strategic transport needs). Their border is crossed by numerous international rivers and watersheds, with lakes, rivers, and streams flowing in both directions. They share four international Great Lakes (and some Canadians would argue a fifth, Lake Michigan). They share great oceanic areas and currents such as the Bay of Fundy–Gulf of Maine, the Beaufort Sea, and the Pacific coastal regions of Washington–British Columbia–Alaska, along with all of the rich fish and navigational values and pollution costs one can encounter in these areas. They share the cold northerly air masses of winter, the warm tropical air masses of summer, and the weather systems and pollutant concentrations (including acid rain) they carry. Finally they share an exceedingly long and diverse border of forests, prairies, mountains, tundras, occasional cities, and boundary waters.

These are geographic realities that all North Americans must accept. With so much transborder contact, the opportunity for conflict is inherently great, as is the need to avoid, or reduce and resolve, that conflict—a continuous process that must be ongoing at all times. The forced sharing of these continental commons and the continuing problems that sharing entails arise naturally from the countries' proximity and intimacy. Nothing can be done about the former and, in practice, little can be done about the latter.

The second concern, military defense, receives little attention because, if anything, it is even more taken for granted by both peoples than are other aspects of the bilateral relationship. Once again, Canada is thrown into a mutual sphere with the United States and is left with little choice in the matter. On the positive side, Canada's national defense in a turbulent world is provided for by its larger neighbor automatically, as a part of the United States' own defense requirements, and at little cost to Canada. Canada can afford to devote a smaller portion of its resources to armaments simply because the United States devotes so much of its own.

Negatively, however, the size of the U.S. defense budget effectively deprives Canada of any real say in its own defense policy (a continuing sore point with some Canadians). Its participation in NATO, NORAD, and a number of other continental defense endeavors is always shaped under the shadow of U.S. decision making. Canada is, of course, free to build up its own defense establishment and military forces (and indeed is encouraged to do so by the United States—some Americans argue that Canada does not "pull its weight" in its own or continental defense). However, all defense decisions of real consequence are made by the United States for the continent as a whole.

No aspect of U.S.–Canadian military relations, of course, assumes the existence of any military threat between the countries. That danger ended in the last century. There are, however, military issues in conflict, especially in national views toward and claims upon the Arctic. The islands and much of the seabed and surface waters of the Arctic on this side of the North Pole are claimed by Canada, both through historic claims of sovereignty dating from the era of British dominion and, more recently in 1970, through the passage of the Arctic Waters Pollution Prevention Act and similar statutes.

The United States, however, does not recognize these claims and, in the interests of strategic and military concerns, asserts that most of these Arctic waters are international and thus open to the passage of U.S. naval surface ships and submarines and oil and gas tankers. The United States has, with its nuclear submarine capacity, been able to make much more effective use of these waters than has Canada, a matter of no little consequence in the interpretation of international law. Ironically, the U.S. challenge to Canadian sovereignty in this region may deny Canada's exclusive control—thus denying the right of exclusive control to a friendly power—while opening up these waters to the free passage of vessels of unfriendly nations. Thus, U.S. claims of international territoriality may not be in the best strategic interests of either the United States or Canada.

The third underestimated characteristic of the bilateral relationship occasionally causes diplomatic problems but would present benefits and opportunities in the best interests of both nations if accepted and put to good use. Canada often enjoys good relations with nations unfriendly to the United States, nations that for political reasons cannot or do not have good relations (or any relations) with the United States. One role it can undertake is as a valuable go-between and alternate window on the world for the United States.

Canada can use its good offices to help the United States better understand the viewpoints of disagreeing allies as well as those of obviously unfriendly nations. As an increasingly important actor on the world stage, Canada can help secure world peace. Furthermore, more internationalist Canada's special relations with less developed nations, with some of which the United States does not have close ties, can be invaluable to the United States and to the interests of world peace. The same can be said of Canada's special relationships with the vast French-speaking world, relationships developed and maintained through Francophone Canadians and reaching into numerous nations in Africa, Asia and the Caribbean. These are relationships, in fact, which Americans cannot readily enjoy.

Canada is in an enviable position and should be quick to embrace the opportunities this position offers. The United States should be equally quick to recognize and make use of these opportunities presented to it by this nation on its northern doorstep.

Canadians and Americans live together and share a continental resource base because they must. The defense of that resource base in a turbulent world has been assumed by the United States, relieving Canada of considerable expense (an expense viewed by many Canadians as of questionable value.) At the same time Canada enjoys a special position among nations, in a world much in need of good will. The United States and Canada can be the breadbasket for a hungry world and a strong voice for human rights. These two democracies are the best equipped to form a potent force in tackling the problems identified in the on-going North-South debate between developed and underdeveloped nations, between "haves" and "have-nots." Whether they can rise above their special interest economic confrontations to accept this bigger challenge so necessary to the survival of the free world is an as yet unresolved question.

Note

1. Cited in *Winston S. Churchill, His Complete Speeches 1897–1963,* ed. by Robert Rhodes James (New York: Chelsea House Publishers, 1974), Vol. 6, p. 6105. Reprinted with permission.

3 Each Other's Best Customer

Ask most Americans who is the United States' largest trading partner and they would probably answer Japan. This is not surprising because Americans drive so many Japanese cars, use so many Japanese television sets, and hear analyses of Japan's economy coupled to statistics about the disruption caused to U.S. industry by too many imports.

Yet U.S. two-way trade with Canada is greater by two-thirds than with Japan, which is our number-two trading partner. Each year Canada buys goods from the United States valued as much as U.S. shipments to the entire European Community. The early 1980s saw Canadian exports to the United States reach the $45 billion level and U.S. exports to Canada reach $47 billion. Canada is by far the United States' largest and most important trading partner.

Much of this trade with Canada is not readily identifiable to the man on the street. About one-fourth of it has been in automobiles, trucks, and auto parts bearing the names of the big three U.S. automakers. The rest is in natural gas, electricity, chemicals, machinery, minerals, forest products, food products and so on—an almost endless list of goods that quickly become integrated in both societies.

The Benefits

Americans are bombarded with facts about the balance of trade deficits and the need to increase foreign trade. But how many realize that the United States and Canada already enjoy the largest trading relationship of any two countries in the world? More than 20 percent of all U.S. foreign exports go to Canada. Of equal significance is the nearly 20 percent of U.S. imports that also come from Canada. Reciprocally, the huge U.S. market is far more important to Canada than it is to any other nation, accounting for nearly 70 percent of all of Canada's foreign trade.

Automotive products, machinery, and equipment make up the largest segment of Canadian exports to the United States. Next in importance are the raw materials of crude oil, natural gas, iron ore and concentrates. Asbestos has also been important. The third category is the fabricated materials of lumber, wood pulp, newsprint, iron and steel and alloys, aluminum and alloys, copper, nickel, and zinc. Fertilizers, the basic chemical products exported to the United States, are fourth with food products trailing the list.

The United States enjoys approximately 70 percent of its Canadian export trade in a wide range of end-products, with some one-half of this volume in automotive products. The rest is in industrial machinery, farm machinery, tractors, aircraft and parts, computers, communication equipment, medical equipment, and consumer items. Fabricated materials make up the second most important U.S. export to Canada and consist largely of forest products, fabric and textile materials, chemicals, petroleum and coal products, metals and alloys. The remaining U.S. exports are coal, other crude materials, and food products consisting largely of fruits, vegetables, and meats.

Other important and growing aspects of the U.S.-Canadian economic relationship have been permanent investments, tourism, travel, and other financial transactions (although to a much lesser extent). The 1980s were ushered in with more than $40 billion of direct U.S. investment in Canada. Lost somewhat in the thinking of Americans is the significance of the approximately $10 billion of direct Canadian investment in the United States, quietly making Canada our third largest foreign investor. Factoring in the 10-to-1 population ratio, often used to compare U.S. and Canadian statistics, shows that Canadians are substantially out-investing their U.S. counterparts. In 1981 the direct per capita investment approximated $500 from Canada compared to $209 from the United States. (Canada screens U.S. investment through the Foreign Investment Review Agency, which will be discussed later. The United States does not similarly screen Canadian investment, although some members of Congress periodically introduce such legislation, often as a retaliatory measure.)

In the area of "nonmerchandise trade," tourism has an increasingly important role to play (especially in Canada, which derives one-fourth of its foreign income from tourism). Some 77 million Canadians and Americans cross the border each year. Many of them are on daily visits or shopping trips, but an estimated 12 million Americans make their stay in Canada for one night or longer, with 10 million Canadians visiting the United States for similar periods. In another area of nonmerchandise trade, Canadian businesses and crown corporations are substantial borrowers from U.S. money markets. These figures manifest another important "silent element" of the U.S.-Canadian economic relationship.

The Problems

The U.S.-Canadian economic relationship is a complex one of dependence and interdependence, and the fruits of being the largest trading partners in the world also bring certain bitters. When economic conditions are bad in the United States, Canada is usually harder hit because, among other reasons, it lacks the economic resilience that size and diversity bring. When the U.S. dollar shrinks, the Canadian dollar weakens. When U.S. interest rates rise, they rise even higher in Canada; and a U.S. recession is almost sure to bring on a Canadian recession, if not a depression. Unemployment is an even more visible index than interest rates: when unemployment rises in the United States, it rises more in Canada, invariably provoking calls for protectionism and greater tariff protection. These measures, if instituted, would only worsen the depressed economic conditions and create bitter feelings among the peoples of both countries.

Being neighbors as well as the largest and seventh largest industrialized nations in the world, the United States and Canada share both benefits and problems that effect—but are not related to—their relationship. In the late 1960s to early 1970s, few observers could have predicted what the 1980s would bring. At that time both the United States and Canada had enjoyed many years of real income gains on the order of 4 or 5 percent per year. Each of them was economically healthy, and people in both countries were optimistic that governments had the ability to solve deep social problems quickly without too much cost to individuals. But the beginning of the 1980s brought change in the form of new and painful realities, realities that were presaged by the high inflation of the late 1970s.

Traditional monetary and fiscal policy tools were proving to be of only limited effectiveness, in the short run, against market powers such as OPEC. Both countries were suddenly hit with slow economic growth and high rates of inflation. They began to experience a new, or perhaps a newly discovered, problem—that of the loss of "productivity." A general cut in worldwide tariffs opened the Canadian and U.S. economies to competition from the newly industrializing countries outside of North America. The world had become effectively less bipolar, and both countries became increasingly aware that they no longer lived in isolation from world economic pressures. Both governments were under increased external pressures from those developing countries who needed and were demanding access to our markets for finished goods.

The impact of this trade has hit specific firms, industries, and regions. Marked shifts in the locus of economic activity have been taking place in both the United States and Canada, shifts that involve a relocation away from the traditional eastern and central areas toward the west in Canada and toward the south and west in the United States. All of these elements—a world of lower tariffs, competition from industrializing countries, and regional shifts—have created pressures on both governments for more interventionist policies to limit adjustment costs and to meet the desire of workers to continue to live in their home areas and work for their same employer or industry.

These are the conditions that spawn tax incentives, subsidies, and other governmental actions to attract and keep industry at home. Such efforts by both governments have created the potential for conflict across the border, a potential that has been fulfilled. The most commonly used tool to control trade has been the application of tariffs, often to discourage trade. The tariff barriers, or the method of applying those tariffs, are a frequent cause of complaint from the business community.

Canada's tariff policy is founded on the National Policy of 1879, which was a policy designed to form a protected national market, encourage western settlement, and strengthen the new Canadian Confederation in order to make it more independent of the United States. This policy obviously did not prevent the growth of trade interdependence; and there has been a resultant dismantling and reduction of tariffs since, with the exception of a period in the early 1930s when they rose to their highest point in response to the protectionist sentiment of the Great Depression.

Completed in 1979, the latest round of multilateral trade negotiations, which will be discussed later, made giant strides toward the removal of trade restrictions between the two countries. This reduction took place through a long series of international conferences held under The General Agreement on Tariffs and Trade (GATT). Besides this function of reducing trade barriers, the GATT and its committees were charged with the equally important task of providing an ongoing overall framework for the resolution of new problems and the settlement of trade disputes. In so doing, GATT will contribute to a climate of greater certainty for international traders, whose confidence in market reliability is a fundamental prerequisite to expanded trade.

Tariffs, however, are not the sole concern of Canadian and U.S. trading partners. Strong feelings of protectionism remain in both countries, embodied in the form of a variety of nontariff measures that require continued discussions by trade officials of both countries. Government procurement policy is an example of one such nontariff trade barrier. The federal governments have "buy Canada" or "buy American" policies for various goods and services, as do some of the states and provinces, that, in effect, restrict trade. Many complaints of "buy Canada" legislation have been voiced by the United States, but it is unrealistic to expect liberalization of government procurement procedures to be unilateral. Canada finds the large number of states with "buy American" statutes to be equally offensive by depriving Canada of needed markets; but, as in other areas, the policies and jurisdictions of provinces, states, and local authorities often prevent federal governments from making a commitment to end such practices.

Another troublesome trade issue has been the "incentives race" to attract new or keep existing industry. It is of particular concern in areas experiencing grave economic difficulty and, again, is difficult to control because the states, provinces, and municipalities involved are operating within their own areas of jurisdiction. Overall, real net economic advantages are difficult to demonstrate from the use of incentives; frequently only successful corporations who know that there are areas on both sides of the border bidding for their presence end up being subsidized. Nonetheless, this new form of international competition is, in many ways, as restrictive as a protective tariff.

It would be unrealistic to expect that there will not always be trade issues between the United States and Canada to occupy the time of government negotiators, garner headlines, and affect the health of the bilateral relationship. At the beginning of the decade of the 1980s, three trade issues emerged as the most prominent in bilateral relations, namely, trade imbalance within the Auto Pact (favoring the United States), Canada's Foreign Investment Review Agency (FIRA), and Prime Minister Trudeau's National Energy Program (NEP) (both favoring Canada). Policies of President Reagan's administration conflicted with those of Pierre Trudeau's government, causing the latter two issues (FIRA and the NEP) to become symbolically, if not directly, responsible for the crumbling of U.S.-Canadian relations.

The U.S.-Canadian Auto Pact was adopted in 1965 in response to an economic need. Auto manufacuring firms had been attracted to Canada years before because of high Canadian tariffs. Production runs in Canada were shorter and costs higher than for the same cars in the United States, so that autos made in Canada for the smaller Canadian market were more expensive to consumers than were autos in the United States. Instead of imposing more trade restrictions, the two countries agreed to expand trade by eliminating tariffs and by encouraging specialization. The Auto Pact created duty-free trade in finished vehicles and automotive parts between the two countries.

This arrangement worked well until 1979. Canadian auto exports rose from 4 percent to nearly 17 percent during the period 1965 to 1979, auto-worker employment in Canada grew from 71,000 jobs to 121,000, and two-way trade in this industry grew from $700 million in 1964 to over $20 billion in 1979. The agreement then turned somewhat sour as the effects of a troubled North American auto industry were felt. Canada, while facing layoffs of its autoworkers similar to those in the United States, also faced a detrimental 1979 trade imbalance in the Auto Pact of over $3 billion.

This imbalance, coupled with Canadian fears that new investments and adjustments needed to meet competition from auto production and consumption in other countries would be made in the United States (leaving Canada with little of the industry), raised the U.S.-Canadian Automotive Agreement again as a major trade issue. Rational voices have expressed the view that real opportunity for success could be enjoyed by combining U.S.-Canadian efforts so as to compete in a cooperative way as a North American industry. For this to occur, however, it would be essential for the dominant

U.S. segment of the industry to go out of its way to guarantee equal treatment and showing of the profits, the losses, and the opportunities. Otherwise, the people of both countries will be the losers in this important industry.

While the future of the Auto Pact has been a major Canadian concern, the proposed changes in the Foreign Investment Review Act and the National Energy Program have occupied U.S. concerns. Canadians remain nervous over and sensitive to excessive U.S. control of Canadian businesses. With some 56 percent of its manufacturing industries under foreign control, the Canadian government in 1974 created the FIRA and charged it with the responsibility of reviewing, for approval or disapproval, proposals by foreign firms for mergers, acquisitions, and new investments in Canada. The crucial criterion for approval is whether the new proposal will be of "significant benefit to Canada. That benefit is generally interpreted to include:

> "employment; the effect of competition within an industry on productivity, efficiency, technological development and product variety in Canada; the degree of significance of participation by Canadians in the business and in any industry of which it would form a part; and the compatibility of the acquisition or establishment with national and economic policies, taking into consideration policy objectives of the government or any province likely to be significantly affected."[1]

Few applications to FIRA are actually rejected. However, U.S. interests argue that they are forced to make too many concessions during the negotiation process and that many such concessions constitute unfair treatment. It is unknown how many potential investors never apply (and never invest) because of the existence of FIRA.

The greatest U.S. quarrel concerning FIRA came over Canadian proposals to conduct a performance review of existing foreign-controlled firms to determine if such companies were operating for "the benefit of Canada." This action, which some investors perceived as a threat, proved to be made of more rhetoric than substance; but it opened the door for strong U.S. objections to a distasteful business concept.

A more legitimate U.S. concern has been the possible FIRA demand that approved firms buy certain needed items or components from Canadian sources, negating agreements reached under the General Agreement on Tariffs and Trade. A further U.S. complaint involves an "extraterritorial" application required by FIRA in cases where a merger or acquisition is taking place outside of Canada and where a Canadian subsidiary is involved. The United States contests FIRA's right to rule on whether the Canadian subsidiary may be retained.

In practice, FIRA has posed few major problems. The threat of possible policy changes is what makes some U.S. business interests uneasy, though one Canadian defense suggests that the United States would respond in a similar negative fashion to such a high degree of foreign ownership and control, particularly in vital industries. From these disagreements one characteristic of the U.S.-Canadian economic relationship has become clear: there exist two worlds—one of rhetoric and the other of substance, a pragmatic functioning system. Neither side may always like what the other is doing or saying, but both seek and find accommodations, for no other reason than that it is in the best interests of each to do so.

The harshest criticism of Canadian policy to come from the United States in many years has centered around the adoption of NEP, announced in October, 1980, and designed to "Canadianize" a greater portion of Canada's rich gas and oil industry. Canada argues that 70 percent of its oil industry is owned and controlled by U.S.-controlled multinational oil companies. Under the NEP, Canada has set forth to increase Canadian ownership and control to 50 percent by the year 1990.

This 50 percent ownership goal would be accomplished by strengthening the government-owned oil company, Petro-Canada (PETROCAN), by providing it with more favorable incentives, and by raising its ability to acquire the assets of private companies. Second, the NEP would alter the price structure, tax structure, and tax incentives for developments taking place on provincial lands in such a manner as to create increased development of federal lands. The third element of the program would increase direct funding to Petro-Canada for the retroactive acquisition of a 25 percent interest in gas and oil already discovered on lands leased from the government. Because costs expended for nonproductive exploration would not be considered, U.S. interests argue that the 25 percent acquisition would be accomplished at far below the original costs, and thus below fair market value.

One of the frequent arguments raised in the United States against the Canadianization of the Canadian oil industry is that because the U.S. industry made the major contribution in developing Canada's energy resources, it is entitled to fairer treatment as its reward. Much of that argument is formalized in Canada's membership in the Organization for Economic Cooperation and Development (OECD) investment code. This code sets forth the principle of nondiscriminatory treatment for established foreign investors. The U.S. multinational oil companies, backed by many U.S. government officials, have charged that the NEP is laden with the discrimination opposed by the OECD and should not be practiced by OECD members.

Canada is the only industrialized nation in the world that has sufficient resources to become energy self-sufficient by the end of this century. From a Canadian viewpoint this fact, coupled with the energy cost escalations imposed by OPEC since 1973, would seem to make a decisive energy policy vital to the future interests of Canada. Here the United States finds itself in a dilemma. Canadianization of such a scarce and vital resource, in effect "being taken" from the most powerful private U.S. interests, is not unpopular

among the Canadian people. Ironically, therefore, the greater the U.S. rhetoric, the more Canadian support is created for a program that is not neces-
sarily popular in all parts of Canada.

The United States has other important energy arrangements with Canada. It already buys some 5 percent of its natural gas there and needs more.
U.S. interests are also involved with Canada in attempts to construct natural
gas pipelines, such as the ALCAN Highway line from Prudhoe Bay, Alaska,
south through Canada to the lower forty-eight states. For reasons of high
interest rates and energy surplus, this pipeline is now on hold. (This one
project would involve an estimated 36 trillion cubic feet of natural gas over a
twenty-five year period and provide access to 12 percent of U.S. natural gas
reserves—in Alaska.) Large discoveries of natural gas in the Canadian
Atlantic provinces have stimulated new transmission plans for the northeastern United States. In addition, Canada has a growing surplus of hydroelectricity and hydro capacity for possible export, and continues to engage in
petroleum swaps that are beneficial to certain regions of both countries. (Of
all the potential trade items involved between our two countries, energy is
one of the most promising and, because of its importance, will be discussed
in detail in a later chapter.)

Any final analysis must question whether either the United States or
Canada can afford to jeopardize their entire rich relationship over single
economic issues, ones that could be quietly resolved, simply to satisfy powerful domestic economic forces. To some observers, the resolution of problems
surrounding FIRA and the NEP would signal a return to a healthy relationship characterized by the kind of everyday issues that result from vigorous
competition within the private sector and in no way evince any real strain.
The economic rewards of past cooperation have been extensive for both
countries. The future holds even greater promise if the United States is
willing to fulfill the role of the larger neighbor toward a smaller and to adopt
a more sensitive and positive stance toward Canada's needs.

The Opportunity

By 1974 cross-border trade between the United States and Canada had
reached $40 billion and seven years later that amount had reached more than
$92 billion. There are indicators that suggest that trade will continue to
escalate on this scale; at the same time, a number of government policies of a
protectionist nature severely threaten that possibility.

One positive indicator is that by the year 1987, when the latest round of
multilateral trade negotiations (MTN) have been fully implemented, tariff
and nontariff barriers between the United States and Canada will have been
substantially reduced. Reductions on the order of 33 percent will create

tremendous opportunities for new trade. For the Canadian export of industrial products, U.S. tariffs will be cut 41 percent, with a final average U.S. rate on dutiable industrial Canadian goods of about 2.8 percent. The comparable Canadian final rate will be about 8.5 percent. Eventually, under these negotiations, close to 85 percent of all Canadian exports to the United States will enter duty free, as will 75 percent of U.S. exports to Canada. Although the results of the MTN are also available to other nations, this application is on a most-favored-nation basis. American companies therefore have a tremendous geographic advantage in exporting to Canada and vice-versa.

Of equal importance, perhaps, are the nontariff agreements that were made. It has long been recognized as a general principle of international trade that, where it is necessary to protect domestic production against imports, the protection should be in the form of tariffs rather than by other protective devices. The MTN put considerable emphasis on reducing the effect of growing nontariff barriers.

Accordingly, the United States, Canada, and our major trading partners also made a number of important agreements on nontariff barriers. New trade codes were agreed to, and corresponding GATT committees were established to ensure that the new rules would be effectively observed by the signatory parties. Among the categories liberalized were subsidies and countervailing duties, anti-dumping duties, product standards and other technical barriers to trade, import licensing procedures, customs valuation, and government procurement.

Finally, this historic round of multilateral trade negotiations holds out the promise of providing the experience and opportunity for further trade liberalization. The MTN agreements raise the question, once again, whether Canada can take the final step and institutionalize total bilateral free trade.

Free trade has been an intriguing issue since the beginning of two-way trade between the United States and Canada. Canada's 1854 Reciprocity Treaty with the United States established reciprocal abolition of duties on nearly all products of farms, forests, mines, and fisheries traded between Nova Scotia and the United States and remained in force until Canadian confederation when protectionism returned. As recently as 1982, the Canadian Senate's Standing Committee on Foreign Affairs came to the following conclusion after an extensive study:

> The committee therefore reaffirms the conclusion reached in its Volume II Report (June 1978) that the desired restructuring, growth and competitiveness of Canadian industry can best be achieved by the negotiation of a bilateral free trade agreement with the United States.[2]

On the United States' side, the Trade Act of 1974 included the authority for the United States to negotiate a "regional" free trade agreement. The

Trade Act of 1979 required the executive branch to perform a study of the feasibility of creating a free trade area among the United States, Mexico, and Canada. This idea, promoted in 1979 by presidential candidates Reagan, Kennedy, and Brown, was instantly unpopular in both Mexico and Canada; it is dismissed in those countries as a ploy by which the United States can gain greater access to Mexican and Canadian oil and gas resources. Nor is bilateral free trade likely to be, pragmatically, a realistic alternative. If free trade between the United States and Canada is to become a reality, it will be achieved through a continued removal of tariffs and nontariff trade barriers, as is being accomplished under the MTN and GATT.

Another viable concept is an expansion of sectoral free-trade arrangements between Canada and the United States, such as the Auto Pact and the Defense Production Sharing Arrangement. Under such arrangements, free trade is allowed on an industry by industry basis. Complete bilateral free trade between the United States and Canada is viewed as simply too risky by many Canadians, who believe the United States would not treat Canada fairly and would simply further dominate the available markets. Gradual step-by-step movement toward free trade has had good results, however, and is proving to be a logical and welcome compromise to these fears.

It should be readily evident that, in an economic relationship of this magnitude, new opportunities are far-ranging and often not obvious. As in the case of the automobile industry, the original bilateral competition has been transformed into serious competition between a North American industry and those in third countries. Greater cooperation between the United States and Canada is an important means of preserving and expanding the trade of certain products of importance to both countries. One suggestion is the so-called Global Product Mandate, which would create world-scale industries that marketed products world-wide rather than by restricting sales to one market. Implementation would involve both increased product specialization in some industries and greater cooperation between the countries in other industries. Greater Canadian-U.S. cooperation would be a step in this direction while Canadian-U.S. failure to cooperate due to their similarities and existing economic interdependence would be a step in the opposite direction.

Research and development is another important area for government encouragement and cooperation. A popular view in Canada is that U.S. industry retains too large a share of the benefits of research and development and leaves its subsidiaries in Canada as largely assembly facilities. Canadians would like more of the research and development activity of U.S. firms doing business in Canada to be conducted in their country, as a means of providing greater growth and skills for Canadian industry as a whole.

Besides this political benefit of relocating industrial research and development, there is a bilateral economic one. Both the United States and

Canada acknowledge that current levels of research and application of new technologies must be greatly increased to make the improvements in productivity so badly needed in both countries and meet third-country competition. Canadian and U.S. expertise working together will result in a stronger North American position in relation to the rest of the world.

Conclusion

It is a truism that both Canada and the United States have the ability to seriously harm one another economically. This fact alone, some believe, insures that the two countries will remain good neighbors. While this position may have been valid in the past, and even to some degree today, nevertheless, the truth is that U.S. responses to this trading partnership over the years have left Canadians with continuing feelings of uneasiness and concern.

In 1970, Prime Minister Trudeau initiated a "third option" plan designed to increase trade with Japan and the European Community; the plan was intended to reduce U.S. trade and consequently Canadian economic vulnerability to the United States. Again, the gravitational pull of U.S. markets proved too great, and this initiative was not destined to achieve the desired result; but it is indicative of a dissatisfied customer and neighbor, a circumstance that should be readily apparent and not go unheeded in the United States.

Dependence on the status quo to maintain a high level of bilateral economic activity will result in a course of lost opportunities, which neither country can afford. As of this writing, the United States has embarked on a course that not only fails to maintain the desirable aspects of the status quo but is moving dangerously close to the destruction of much of the bilateral economic progress already achieved. Writing in a recent issue of *Foreign Affairs*, Canadian author Marie Josée Drouin and U.S. economist Harald B. Malmgren warned:

> Relations between Canada and the United States have become more strained than at any time in recent memory. There have been many earlier periods of tension, but the policy orientations of the two capitals in late 1981 appear to be far more divergent than in the past. The two governments seem to be on a collision course, in a context that political leaders cannot fully control.... The special relationship no longer seems to have meaning. The rhetoric of recent policy statements by U.S. officials has openly condemned Canadian economic policies, and in reply Canadians have accused the United States of bullying Canada and of trying to prevent Canadians from asserting their independence and achieving autonomous development of their own economy.[3]

These are serious observations, but they are being made by growing numbers of people on both sides of the border who are familiar with U.S.-Canadian relations.

Whether irreparable harm has been done to this unique trading relationship is not yet clear. Nor is it clear whether the United States will ever recognize Canada as its largest and most important trading partner and act accordingly. Surely, however, if the United States fails to recognize the latter reality, the chances for irreparable harm are increased.

Notes

1. U.S. Department of Commerce, Industry and Trade Administration, *Overseas Business Reports: Marketing in Canada* (Washington: U.S. Department of Commerce, November, 1979), p. 24.

2. Senate of Canada, Standing Committee on Foreign Affairs, *Canada-United States Relations,* vol. 3, "Canada's Trade Relations with the United States," Summary III, 1982.

3. Marie-Josée Drouin and Harald B. Malmgren, "Canada, The United States and the World Economy," excerpted by permission of *Foreign Affairs,* 60, No. 2 (Winter 1981/82): 393, 395. Copyright 1982 by the Council on Foreign Relations, Inc.

4 Sharing Continental Concerns

At any given time, the top ten items on the list of irritants on the U.S.-Canadian diplomatic agenda includes a number of transboundary environmental issues.[1] The list also invariably contains one or more fishery disputes, water resource questions of one sort or another, and occasionally conflict over disputed maritime boundary claims. All of these issues have one thing in common: they are invariably perceived as local or regional, and thereby inconsequential, by Americans, and they are often treated as national issues involving great national pride and honor (and often national values) by Canadians. This difference in approach alone is sufficient to exacerbate the bilateral seriousness of these issues and insure a place for them on the diplomatic agenda. All of these issues ultimately stem from the necessity, as described in chapter 2, of sharing the continental commons, the common watersheds and drainage basins, the common air masses, and the common seas and all that is in them.

Transboundary Environmental Problems

Bilateral disputes over the allocation of boundary and near-boundary water resources and air masses are not new phenomena on the U.S.-Canadian scene, as the long record of debates over the Great Lakes levels and pollution concerns and the competition for scarce water resources on the prairies indicate. Indeed, it was precisely these two areas of concern that led to the late nineteenth-century formation of the International Waterway Commission and by 1911 its successor, the International Joint Commission. As near-border economic development intensified, the foundation was laid for escalating conflict, culminating in the extensive scope of environmental conflict we witness today.

The Boundary Waters Treaty of 1909 and the treaty's vehicle for implementation, the International Joint Commission (IJC), have built a foundation that has underlain bilateral environmental relations between Canada and the United States for nearly three-quarters of a century. Touted worldwide as a unique model of what can be accomplished by two nations with sufficient will, the treaty and the commission have long been respected for their unusual spirit of collegiality; for their long record of sound scientific and technical findings; for the unique nature of their organization and approaches; and, perhaps most significantly, for their success in conflict avoidance. Recognition on all of these grounds is justified, though a caveat is in order: the commission's task under the treaty has been narrow and specialized; its work has been relegated to noncontroversial areas where there was already diplomatic recognition that agreement could be achieved; and most of its efforts, especially in recent years, have led to nonbinding recommendations that the two governments can (and often do) ignore. Hence the work of this in many respects admirable treaty and vehicle is confined and its impact limited.

The Boundary Waters Treaty established the rules and procedures by which boundary waters (including waters flowing across as well as those forming the boundary) would be allocated in relation to upstream and downstream interests and among various categories of users. The IJC's decisions in this area are binding. The treaty also provided a vehicle whereby the two federal governments could refer matters (in theory any matters, but in practice mainly air and water pollution matters) to the IJC for nonbinding recommendations and advice. This aspect of its mandate has occupied most of the commission's time in recent years.

The treaty governs U.S.-Canadian interaction over the Great Lakes, ranging from lake level matters of great consequence to hydroelectric power, navigation, and shoreline impacts to water pollution questions in the lakes (all except Lake Michigan, which is not considered international and therefore is not under the purview of the treaty) and their connecting channels (St. Marys, St. Clair, Detroit, and Niagara rivers and the St. Lawrence). In fact, the 1909 treaty even uses the word pollution, which was unusual at that early date but a reflection of the early pollution concerns in portions of the lakes and connecting channels, particularly in the Detroit and St. Clair rivers. Since its earliest origins, the IJC has devoted a major portion of its work to water quality in the lakes; it was, for example, involved in an intense period of pollution investigation, analysis, and surveillance, especially in Lakes Erie and Ontario (the "lower lakes"), culminating in the Great Lakes Water Quality Agreements of 1972 and 1978.

The commission was given principal responsibility for implementing the conditions of these two agreements and established a Great Lakes Regional Office at Windsor, Ontario, to carry out this task. Pollution in Lakes Erie and Ontario peaked in the early 1970s and reductions in overall pollution have been recorded in recent years. However, the nature of the lakes' pollution has changed from the more conventional municipal sewerage and industrial effluent to much more unconventional and difficult to manage toxic substances. These substances, especially in the Niagara River, are now emerging as a particularly difficult bilateral dispute—one which is certainly exacerbated by the dramatic Reagan administration budget cuts for the U.S. Environmental Protection Agency, the lead federal agency in water quality and through the 1970s a major presence on the lakes.

The true impact of the Boundary Waters Treaty and the IJC on water quality in the Great Lakes is yet to be assessed. Clearly, the lakes would not be cleaner without this bilateral involvement. Whether they would be dirtier without that involvement is not as certain. There is no doubt, however, that the efforts of the IJC under the treaty have informed millions of people in both countries of the lakes' problems; that there are serious threats to the water quality of the upper lakes (Huron and Superior) which were thought to be safe; and that scientists from both governments can work well together in generating data and presenting findings acceptable to both sides. The blame for continuing deterioration of the lakes may well, therefore, be placed at the feet of those in government and elsewhere in the two societies who have the responsibility of receiving this data and acting on it. One thing is certain: serious pollution in the Great Lakes does not result from the sharing of the lakes by two countries. This pollution would exist, at the very least at present levels, even if the lakes were wholly contained within one nation. It cannot be said that the lakes suffer from being an international "no man's land." Indeed, they have received increased attention because of their international status and may be the better for that attention today.

The scarcity of water and particularly potable water in the U.S.-Canadian international prairie region has also provided a setting for transboundary environmental disputes. On the dry prairies the countless small rivers and streams take on an image larger than life, at least by the standards of those living in well-watered areas. Hence, those used to water abundance wonder at the seriousness of disputes, highlighted by diplomatic headlines, over such water sources as the Poplar River (site of a Saskatchewan coal-fired power plant), the Souris River (embroiled in the great Garrison irrigation dispute), the Red River (with its chronic pollution and flooding problems), and such tiny prairie streams as the Pembina and the St. Mary. Greatest among the prairie disputes are the Poplar and Garrison issues, both of which have caused political earthquakes in Ottawa and much consternation in Washington.

The government of Saskatchewan's construction of a large (up to 1200 MW) coal-fired power plant and associated coal mines on the Poplar River just a few miles north of the U.S. border offers many benefits to that province, while nothing but costs to adjacent Montana. The Poplar issue is particularly noteworthy in that it is the only transboundary environmental problem to contain all three of these distinct elements: water quantity or apportionment, water quality, and air quality. The operation of the plant presents costs to Montana in all three areas (albeit the extent of those costs are much debated). Water-scarce northeastern Montana begrudges any loss of water rights (even though the Poplar water apportionment settlement increases Montana's water entitlement on other streams). This agricultural region is also concerned about impacts on the quality of its irrigation water and about the effect of air pollutants (from a plant without sulfur pollution controls) on its crops and livestock. Its fears have been heard loudly and clearly in Washington, bringing strong pressure there to resist Canadian plans. The IJC has been actively involved, mitigating the water apportionment and quality aspects of this dispute. There is no question, however, that Montana suffers opportunity costs because of Canada's ability to exercise the western "first in time, first in right" philosophy (which derives from western prior appropriation water-rights doctrine, but which could apply to pollution as well).

In contrast, the Garrison irrigation dispute[2] is well known in Canada but seldom discussed in the United States. In the late 1940s ambitious plans were laid to carry out substantial federal manipulation of the waters of the dry Missouri Basin. Part of this plan included the large-scale diversion of the Missouri River into the northward-flowing Souris–Red River–Hudson Bay drainage, thereby irrigating (and substantially revolutionizing the future of) central and eastern North Dakota. The great Garrison debate, very much a U.S. domestic environmental issue aside from its bilateral ramifications, was the result.

Along with providing much additional water to the farms, municipalities, and (hopefully) industries of North Dakota, this diversion from a Gulf of Mexico to an Arctic drainage basin, according to the findings of many scientists and of the IJC, will result in pollution of the Canadian Souris and other rivers north of the border (from agricultural run-off and soil leaching) such that a number of Manitoba communities would be deprived of their only source of water. Perhaps more important, the transfer of Missouri River fish parasites and disease biota into Canada's Lakes Winnipeg and Manitoba would take place, thereby threatening (or even destroying) a well-established commercial fishery and the social fabric of the societies dependent upon that fishery.

Manitoban and Canadian objections to Garrison did not begin as early as they could have; but when they started, they reverberated with great force all across the land, as they still do today. The province of Manitoba, with strong Ottawa backing, has protested loudly and consistently to Washington and to any American audience that would listen. All segments of the Canadian society, including peoples as far removed from Manitoba as Halifax and Vancouver are well versed on Garrison. The media (and particularly editorial writers) have kept this issue in the forefront nation-wide: almost every week the current events surrounding Garrison are debated in the Canadian House of Commons.

Garrison is a classic example of the type of U.S.-Canadian issue that quickly becomes associated with the national interests of Canada but is viewed south of the border (by the few who are even aware of it) as strictly a local or regional issue. Garrison is, of course, a major issue in North Dakota and commands some minor interest in South Dakota and Minnesota; but it is unknown or viewed as of little consequence elsewhere. The true bilateral danger of Garrison is not in water pollution or biota transfer, although those problems are real enough, but rather in the great foreign relations costs of the issue. A whole generation of Canadians is growing up with the Garrison symbol, a symbol in which the United States plays the role of an inconsiderate, uncaring, even bullying country with no regard for the consequences of its actions on a neighboring people, even when the cost of rectifying the problem and avoiding those consequences is small. It is doubtful whether the American people consciously want to assume this image before the Canadian people, but this is what is happening.

Seriously compounding the Garrison issue is the fact that the highly respected and truly bilateral International Joint Commission, after extensive study, has found that to proceed with the project as planned would indeed bring the harm to Canada that that country fears, thereby violating the Boundary Waters Treaty of 1909. To the extent Americans support (or permit) Garrison to go forward, they are helping to maintain their image in Canada as not only an uncaring people but one clearly willing to discard the treaty and all that it represents. In all likelihood Americans would not be so disposed if they realized the consequences of their action. Danger to both peoples thus lies in the ignorance of too many Americans about Canada and its concerns. Until such time as the U.S. Congress and administration agree to significant modification of the project or its repeal, Canadians will insure that it remains a serious bilateral issue and a continuing thorn in the side of the diplomatic relationship.

Serious bilateral environmental problems have also arisen in the coastal marine environment. The Eastport oil refinery controversy on the Atlantic coast has continued for a decade, as Canadian opposition to the siting of a large, proposed oil refinery (100,000 barrels per day) at Eastport, Maine, has intensified over the years. Access to the refinery site involves the transiting of oil-carrying supertankers through Canada's narrow Head Harbor Passage, a navigationally challenging task intensified by severe currents and high fog regimes. At risk in the event of an accident is not only the local marine ecosystem and shorelines but—of great importance to Canada—an increasingly valuable commercial fishery throughout the Bay of Fundy. This dispute is heightened by the U.S. claim of the right of "innocent passage" through these Canadian waters and the Canadian counterclaim that passage of so much oil at such high risk is not "innocent." The debate continues unresolved as the American proponent of the project, the Pittston Company, after gradually obtaining its various permits to begin construction, could not resolve all legal requirements. In Canada the issue, though not as well known nationally as Garrison, is as intensely opposed. The political stakes are high, even though the passage of time may have resolved the debate itself. Foreign relations costs are still being incurred.

On the West Coast there is the issue of U.S. oil tanker transport between Alaska (and perhaps eventually Asia) to Washington State refineries, and the passage of this oil in supertankers through the dangerous and ecologically sensitive waters of the Strait of Juan de Fuca in the vicinity of both Victoria and Vancouver. Although boundary claims are not at issue here, the need for a mandatory vessel traffic management system with bilateral implications has been a part of this dispute. Such a system has been achieved by bilateral agreement; but British Columbians still perceive a significant threat of damage and have kept Ottawa under some pressure.

Air quality disputes have a shorter history than do water-related disputes, being highlighted by the early Trail Smelter controversy in British Columbia–Washington, which is the only bilateral environmental dispute ever to be settled by binding arbitration. Other air quality differences, such as the Michigan–Ontario (Detroit–Windsor and Sarnia–Port Huron) urban-industrial air pollution problems, the Cornwall Island smelter problem (Ontario–New York), and the air quality aspects of the Poplar River power plant (Saskatchewan–Montana), have not ended so decisively. What is clear, however, is that the acid rain issue has emerged into so dominant an issue in the bilateral relationship that all other air quality issues are now being subsumed by these negotiations, discussions that are gradually leading toward a new international air quality treaty or agreement.[3]

The acid rain issue is a giant among all U.S.-Canadian environmental problems and will likely have a long-term impact on the relationship and on how it is conducted in the future. The stage is set for a bilateral problem, given that so much of Canada is geologically highly vulnerable to acid deposition; that a high percentage of all deposition in Canada (at least 50 percent) derives from U.S. sources; and that Canada's forest productivity, a critical factor in the nation's future, may be endangered. The fact that the United States is much less concerned over the seriousness of the issue (as well as significantly less aware); that U.S. vulnerability is probably much less; and that Canada contributes only a small portion (about 15 percent to 20 percent) of U.S. acid deposition creates further imbalance and thus exacerbates the bilateral dispute. The stakes involved in the acid rain debate are economically (and therefore politically) and also quite possibly ecologically much higher than those associated with other bilateral environmental issues. The populations affected, many millions in both countries, include many who live far removed from the international border—people who are experiencing bilateral problems for the first time. The real cost of the acid rain dispute may well be, however, in foreign relations: this is the first environmental issue of a magnitude and consequence sufficient to pose a direct threat to the long-term health of the U.S.-Canadian relationship.

Other such transboundary environmental disputes that have received their share of attention over the years, particularly in the Canadian media, include the Skagit–High Ross Dam issue in Washington–British Columbia; the Atikokan power plant issue in Ontario–Minnesota; the Cabin Creek coal mine issue in British Columbia–Montana; and the Champlain–Richelieu issue in Quebec–Vermont.[4] All of these issues have one characteristic in common: all the benefits accrue on one side of the border, while all the costs accrue on the other. And, because issues cannot in practice be linked or traded off against each other, there is little basis to establish a give and take compromise; resolution of such issues calls for a willingness by the polluter to increase costs so as to protect persons across the border.

The vast majority of U.S.-Canadian transboundary environmental issues are directly energy related, whether derived from power plants or coal mines near the border, hydroelectric dams on transboundary rivers, or oil transport at sea. Many of them have resulted historically from significantly higher levels of both population and industrial development south of the border. In recent years an increasing number have resulted from Canadian plans (and, for the first time, ability) to develop near-border resources with transborder impacts, in what has been called Canada's near-border "development corridor." Some result from a U.S. tendency to designate national parks, wilderness, and wild and scenic rivers in equally near-border locations where they are in the path of pollution crossing the border. Others result from Canada's need to maintain its position in relation to world competition for its resource exports. Still others result from the U.S. drive for energy independence.

For these and other reasons, transboundary environmental conflicts are increasing in number and complexity, are long lasting, and are often not even susceptible to management and containment, much less resolution. Through the Boundary Waters Treaty of 1909 and its Harmon Doctrine (which gives the upstream nation superior water rights), an attempt was made to establish rule and order. Neither nation readily applies the treaty nor uses it to its maximum potential, however; this failure, combined with their inability to act decisively on an international air-quality agreement, has created chaos in the area of transboundary issues. Both peoples will suffer the erosion of their relationship and the loss of future opportunities until they choose to use the means available to resolve these questions and introduce order.

Fishery and Boundary Questions

The Canadian society is in many respects fish oriented. Canada's heritage and culture place a high premium on commercial fishing, fish consumption, and fish export to the world market; and they are thus based upon the allied industries and way of life that such a major national commitment entails. This involvement is characteristic not only of the ocean coasts but also of the provinces with interior waters. Six of Canada's ten provinces have an important interest in commercial marine fishing and two others are committed to inland freshwater commercial fisheries. Furthermore, given this priority scale and Canada's present and future export prospects, Ottawa has begun heavy subsidization and investment in this national fishery, giving all Canadians a much more direct stake in it.

In almost every way, the U.S. society is opposite (even though the total value of the U.S. catch, given greater access to the warm Pacific, Gulf of Mexico, and south Atlantic waters, is higher). Although the fishery was part of New England's heritage, virtually no region of the United States is as oriented toward a fishery heritage and lifestyle or as economically dependent on fish as is so much of Canada. In the United States there is little interest in fish export, a low per capita fish consumption, and limited political support for a national fishery constituency. (New England is an exception, accounting for the unyielding U.S. fishery position regarding negotiation with Canada on a fishing treaty in recent years. Senate opposition to the ratification of that treaty was led by Senators Edward Kennedy of Massachusetts and Claiborne Pell of Rhode Island.) Further, there is very little federal investment in the fishery and little subsidy available. Americans are not about to substitute the sacred cow symbolic of their beef-eating preferences for the once sacred (at least in Boston!) cod.

Hence, fundamental differences in approaches to fish exist within the two countries; and Canada is infinitely more sensitive to threats to its fisheries than the United States, a point not readily understood by Americans. This greater Canadian fishery concern has emerged in the Eastport oil refinery issue, the West Coast oil tanker issue, and even in the inland Garrison Diversion issue. It is in the area of head-to-head conflict over the allocation of fish stocks, however, that the most serious differences have arisen. This situation has been exacerbated by the strong resentment harbored by American fishermen toward their much larger, better equipped, government-subsidized Canadian competitors, a resentment fueled by the ability of those competitors to sell large quantities of their catch to the U.S. market at low prices (benefiting the U.S. consumer but at a cost to U.S. fishermen).

Bilateral fishery disputes have been a continuing feature of U.S.-Canadian relations and have occurred inshore and offshore on both the Atlantic and Pacific coasts, including along both Pacific coast boundary areas, for many years. Arguments over valuable salmon resources on the Washington–British Columbia and British Columbia–Alaska borders have been long-lasting and difficult of resolution; they are aggravated not only by competition for the stock but also through the high level of government investment by both nations in hatchery and fish-ladder facilities. As long as salmon are valuable, as long as they continue to fail to recognize international boundaries, and as long as there continues to be some question as to precisely where those boundaries fall and whose fish belong to whom, these sharp and emotional disputes will continue without resolution. Other Pacific fisheries questions, including those surrounding tuna and groundfish, lend themselves much more readily to resolution—either bilaterally or in the broader multilateral sphere.

The East Coast situation has been less sanguine, in spite of there being only one border. Simmering differences between Canadian and American commercial fishing interests in the Bay of Fundy–Gulf of Maine, and especially on Georges Bank, a very fertile fishing ground, burst into loud and acrimonious debate in 1977; at that time both nations unilaterally extended their seaward boundaries 200 miles, creating a new boundary dispute with an overlapping claim on the critical Georges Bank. This simultaneous unilateral extension had other repercussions: it raised the hopes of New England as well as eastern Canadian fishermen, and these groups (along with the Canadian government) began to significantly increase their level of investment in the Georges Bank fishery, thus raising the future stakes in this dispute and making resolution much more difficult. A reasonably good prospect of achieving joint management of the fishery stocks in question, a condition extant prior to 1977, deteriorated with these rising stakes, the boundary dispute, a hardened political attitude of key New England politicians, and the inability of the weakened Carter administration to achieve necessary treaty ratification in the U.S. Senate. All of these factors coalesced to create what developed into one of the most serious U.S.-Canadian disputes in the late 1970s and early 1980s, ending in a crisis of Canadian confidence in the American people that will persist for some time to come.

The question that Americans must ask is to what extent and how accurately have they calculated the foreign relations costs of this dispute. The issue is much broader than fish; and once again Americans, through ignorance, have failed to recognize the issues of critical importance to Canada. Instead of assessing the whole situation and making a decision, U.S. politicians often seem to act out of ignorance in order to protect a narrow regional interest, thereby damaging their credibility in Canadian eyes. The East Coast fisheries dispute, a dispute that remains unresolved and threatens the economic viability and ecological integrity of one of the finest of North American fisheries, has left a residue of sour relations that will color the ultimate settlement and allocation of the stocks for a long time.

Related to these fisheries issues is the matter of the maritime boundary disputes—sovereignty questions that have arisen largely through the unilateral extension of the offshore 200-mile economic zones. Few Americans are aware of the fact that all four U.S.-Canadian maritime boundaries (Maine–New Brunswick, Washington–British Columbia, Alaska–British Columbia, Alaska–Yukon) are in dispute. These disagreements are most directly concerned with hydrocarbon exploitation: all four areas are thought to have oil and gas reserves. For the present, the Atlantic and Arctic disputes are the most consequential, although the two Pacific disputes involve latent problems.

The Atlantic (Georges Bank) dispute did not inherently affect the fishery, for a joint stock management plan could have been achieved without boundary resolution; nevertheless, the U.S. refusal to work toward this end caused a linkage of fish both to hydrocarbons and the sovereignty question. It also caused an historic referral of this sovereignty dispute to the International Court of Justice (the World Court) at the Hague, a signal to the world that these two nations are unable to achieve resolution alone. It remains to be seen whether the U.S. claim to Georges Bank, based on the location of a deep channel separating the bank from the Nova Scotia mainland, or the Canadian claim, based on equidistance between Nova Scotia and New England, will be granted recognition. At stake are both hydrocarbons and the fishery, for the bitter fishery dispute may preclude access to one nation's portion of the bank by citizens of the other nation.

The Beaufort Sea dispute encompasses a substantial overlapping claim to a sea bottom that is undoubtedly rich in natural gas. The area of disputed territory is wide farther offshore, and relates to differing interpretations of the direction of the international boundary from the mainland to the North Pole. This and the Pacific boundary disputes all result from differing interpretations of early treaties involving the United States, the United Kingdom, and Russia (once sovereign over Alaska). It is possible that these three boundary disputes will take precedence from and ultimately be settled by the findings of the World Court on the Georges Bank dispute. All these disputed boundaries have natural-resource ramifications and, so long as they remain unsettled, preclude resource development.

Water as a Continental Resource

Water sources flowing near the U.S.-Canadian boundary and as resources capable of destruction by pollution have already been discussed. The topic of water as a continental resource still remains. During the 1960s considerable debate concerned the disposition of the continental water resource, in the context of significant American demand and enormous Canadian supply. This dichotomy of demand and supply created opportunity and political controversy, especially in Canada, which often views itself as in the greedy line-of-sight of American "resource-grabbers." Early Canadian discussion of possibly providing water for a thirsty and perhaps well-paying U.S. market suddenly ended with the crafting of the extremely ambitious, controversial, and almost certainly unworkable North American Water and Power Alliance (NAWAPA), a megascale plan (referred to in Canada as a "diabolical plot") to move large quantities of freshwater out of northern Canadian and Alaskan river basins southward through the Rocky Mountain Trench to the arid American Southwest and Mexico. This and other plans for largescale interbasin transfer southward created an intense fear in a Canadian society that felt that water was inextricably linked to Canada's heritage and future independence. These plans were perceived not as opportunities but as tangible threats to the Canadian nation. Such thinking became so implanted in the Canadian psyche that politically such matters are not discussable. Canada does indeed have considerable quantities of unused freshwater in the north (although to term this water wasted is erroneous as it fulfills ecological purposes). The U.S. demand for that water increases yearly. An emerging issue is the "mining" of deep groundwater and the consequent drawdown of aquifers and their pollution, one example being the depletion of the Great Plains groundwater aquifers and the various proposals for coal slurry pipelines, both of which look to the Great Lakes for a necessary water source.

Whether great interbasin transfers are, in real terms, desirable is an open question. Whether Canadian anathema to this question will ever disappear, however, may be a question of equal import. Water was the issue dominant in the 1960s and has been replaced by energy in the years since. Yet there are many observers who say that by the advent of the 1990s, water will again take its place as *the* primary resource question in North America. There is no question that continental demand for water in the coming years of water shortage, especially in the energy-rich West, will keep this issue high on the U.S.-Canadian agenda. It is the responsibility of both peoples to prepare to meet this challenge.

Notes

1. For the definitive work on U.S.-Canadian environmental relations, the reader is referred to John E. Carroll, *Environmental Diplomacy: An Examination and Prospective of Canadian-United States Transboundary Environmental Relations* (University of Michigan Press [U.S.] and John Wiley and Sons, Ltd. [Canada], 1983), 382 pages.

2. An in-depth treatment of the Garrison issue as a bilateral issue can be found in John E. Carroll and Rod Logan, *The Garrison Diversion Unit: A Case Study in Canadian-U.S. Environmental Relations* (Montreal: C.D. Howe Institute, Canada-U.S. Prospects Series, 1980), 52 pp.

3. For an in-depth analysis of acid rain as a bilateral issue, see John E. Carroll, *Acid Rain: An Issue in Canadian-American Relations* (Canadian-American Committee, National Planning Association, 1606 New Hampshire Avenue, N.W., Washington, D.C., 1982). See also John E. Carroll, "Acid Rain Diplomacy," *Alternatives,* 11, No. 2 (1983):

4. For a description of these and other disputes, see John E. Carroll, "When Pollution Knows No Boundaries," *National Parks and Conservation Magazine* 52, no. 3 (1978): 19-24; and "Shadows on the Border," *The Living Wilderness Magazine,* 45, no. 156 (Spring, 1982) 18-22. See also *Environmental Diplomacy,* listed in the first footnote in this chapter.

5 The Challenge of Bilateral Energy Relations

The previous chapter illustrated the fact that most U.S.-Canadian trans-boundary environmental problems are directly energy related. In addition, the broad bilateral environmental problem of acid rain is basically an energy problem south of the border, though increasingly one north of the border. There is another underlying context to U.S.-Canadian energy relations, however, and that is the matter of energy trade. With few exceptions, this trade boils down to Canadian energy export to the United States, to Canadian supply and U.S. market demand. It is these energy and environmental issues, sometimes linked inextricably, that dominate the bilateral agenda, an agenda once heavily weighted with trade and investment matters of a broader genre.

In terms of energy resource wealth, Canada is one of the most well-endowed nations on earth. Its ability to become one of the very few energy self-sufficient industrialized nations in the world is a major cause of a growing feeling of independence. Canada's energy reserves take many forms: hydroelectricity, natural gas, uranium, coal, and, perhaps in somewhat lesser quantities, oil. Market price is, of course, a major determinant of how much of this energy wealth is exploited; but it is there, in the ground, in the rivers, under the sea, awaiting the price sufficient to signal development. Much of Canada has not even been explored yet, leading to the possibility of still greater exploitable energy wealth. All this energy is worth, partly, the cost of its development and transport. More significantly, it is worth whatever people are able and willing to pay. In these post-embargo days, that market price is sufficient to justify very expensive frontier energy development, making Canada a potentially very rich nation. The issue is no longer at what point price will justify development but at what point price and development merge.

Just to the south of this energy-rich land lies a vast and almost insatiable market for energy, a richly endowed nation that is nevertheless heavily dependent upon foreign oil. Its virtual desperation at times to import more oil guarantees prices acceptable to Canada.

A symbiotic relationship springs from these balances of needs and resources. The existence of that relationship is yet another reason for jointly needed cooperation on near-border and boundary area energy development, such as on the Columbia River and the St. Lawrence. It satisfies Canada's need for foreign (usually U.S.) capital to engage in large-scale energy

39

resource development projects, such as James Bay, Churchill Falls, and the Alberta tar sands.

Given the known Canadian supply, the continuing U.S. market, and the economic requirement of binational collaboration, it is not surprising that energy constitutes an important aspect of U.S.-Canadian relations, one that presents particularly complex challenges and opportunities. Energy is also responsible for a number of strains in the relationship, strains that can easily spill over into other facets of the relationship and inhibit opportunities, both in energy and otherwise. The fact remains that America needs Canadian energy and Canada needs the economic benefits from those sales. It is energy that offers the greatest trade opportunity for the future.[1]

Hydroelectricity and Natural Gas: Growth Sectors in Bilateral Energy Relations

The great Canadian wealth in hydroelectricity development and potential development, located largely in Newfoundland-Labrador, Quebec, Manitoba, and British Columbia, coupled with the sudden upsurge in interest in this clean and renewable form of energy, accounts for the important position of hydro, now and especially in future bilateral energy relations. The rapid cost escalation in fossil fuels since the 1974 OPEC embargo and the huge underestimation of the costs of nuclear-generated power, not to mention the intractable health and pollution problems associated with coal, have all made hydro—and even hydro from very distant sources—surprisingly cost competitive. The ambitious and dramatic James Bay (La Grande) Hydro Project in Quebec, with its enormous power potentials (equal to the use of an estimated 600,000 barrels of oil per day—the output of two normal-size oil refineries) has excited the imagination of many North Americans on both sides of the border. Quebec's determination to export this power, as well as that province's desire to assume a world leadership position in both hydro generation and long-distance transmission technology, has served to promote the cause of hydro development, particularly for the demanding northeastern U.S. market. With Quebec's ability to substantially undersell the cost of equivalent electrical generation in that region of the United States the market is vast indeed and holds promise of providing substantial cash flow return to Quebec.[2]

Although slowed by a powerline right-of-way dispute with Quebec, Newfoundland–Labrador also offers great potential for export from Churchill Falls and perhaps eventually from Gull Island, both located in Labrador and in competition with Quebec for the same U.S. markets. Manitoba is just beginning to look seriously at the possibility of export into the U.S. midcontinent region from its many promising sites on the Nelson River and elsewhere in the north. British Columbia with its heavy precipitation and appropriate topography always holds potential for export to the U.S. West

Coast, a still rapidly growing market. Columbia River development, under a 1962 treaty for joint sharing of benefits, may be only the beginning in the western region.

Canada's dream of insuring its own energy independence has led in recent years to the eastward extension of its transcontinental gas distribution system, first from Alberta to Toronto, thence to Montreal and now to Quebec City. Ultimately it may reach Halifax. The purpose is to wean Quebec (and perhaps the Maritime provinces) "off OPEC oil." For the same reasons, the Ottawa government is heavily subsidizing and in all other ways encouraging outer continental shelf gas and oil exploration and development along the Atlantic coast (notably at Sable Island, Nova Scotia, and off Newfoundland and Labrador); at the same time it is pioneering (in a government-private sector partnership) very expensive development in the eastern Canadian Arctic and in the Beaufort Sea. All of these endeavors have a significant (though not often publicized) international export component:

> Construction of a natural gas pipeline from Nova Scotia to southern New England can only be justified by contract for sale of the gas it would carry to the substantial gas export market in the northeastern U.S.

> Outer continental shelf hydrocarbon development on the East Coast is so costly that substantial U.S. investment, private sector investment, is needed; between the current Canadian gas surplus and the quantities of oil required to justify the operation, U.S. markets are inevitable (particularly for the substantial gas reserves already discovered at Sable Island).

> For much the same reasons of project magnitude and gas potential, any Arctic development would be both sizable and beyond the capacity of the Canadian economy to absorb (albeit here export could occur to northern Europe or to Japan rather than to the United States).

Recent incentives have led to the discovery of substantial new natural-gas reserves in Canada. A large "bubble" (surplus) exists today from conventional Alberta and British Columbia fields, from Alberta deep or tight gas (gas at great depth or in tight geological formations), and from outer continental shelf and Arctic finds. The frontiers, which include the Mackenzie Delta regions, the Arctic Islands and the East Coast exploration area from the Baffin Strait to the Scotian Shelf, have estimated natural gas reserves of more than 200 trillion cubic feet, with about 33 trillion cubic feet already discovered. Canada is well endowed with great quantities of natural gas—though it must be noted that gas from other than conventional sources is expensive and thus price dependent. Canadian realization of the existence of this bubble, estimated to be in excess of a thirty-five-year reserve, has led to stepped-up plans for export to the United States: through old existing pipelines in the midcontinent, through the two new sections of the Alaska–Foothills pipelines just completed to California and the Midwest, through new pipeline arrangements across New York State into southern New England, and through repeated calls for a line from New Brunswick across northern and central New England. Potential activity in transborder natural gas movement appears to be considerable.

A significant factor in U.S.-Canadian natural gas relations is the ambitious proposed Alaska–Yukon Foothills natural gas pipeline, whose fate hangs suspended on the resolution of serious financing problems. Just being the largest joint venture ever in the history of the bilateral relationship makes it worthy of mention. This pipeline would initially transport some 12 percent of U.S. natural gas reserves from Alaska to U.S. destinations in the lower forty-eight states (both in the Far West and the Midwest); it would, however, cross a substantial portion of Canadian territory and deeply involve Canadians in many ways. Later, when the Canadian Mackenzie Delta gas reserves are developed, the pipeline would carry Canadian gas to Canadian markets in the south and east. The entire project is based upon a successfully negotiated bilateral treaty and avoids many of the environmental and social concerns associated with other northern pipelines and ventures of great magnitude. The large project cost, the uncertainty over the volume of future gas supplies (and hence the future price), and the generally depressed economy of both nations are currently creating severe financing problems and casting an uncertain cloud over the future of the project. The southern portions of the line are now complete and are currently exporting Alberta gas to the United States, with the expectation that Alaskan gas will ultimately be exported to Canada in the same proportion once the northern section is complete. This agreement could cause significant disruption of bilateral relations, for Canada built the southern portion and is exporting nearly 4 trillion cubic feet over an eight-year period, under the assumption that the United States will build the northern portion and replace the exported gas, if necessary. The U.S. Congress has passed a resolution facilitating the project, but, due to the uncertainty over financing, has not been able to honor its intent.

Two Missed Opportunities

The energy demand situation in the northeastern United States, particularly with respect to oil, has presented Americans with an opportunity to further improve bilateral energy relations with the eastern Canadian provinces. Unfortunately, Americans have not taken advantage of those opportunities, at a cost to both regions.

New England, in spite of its very great oil dependency (nearly 90 percent dependence on fossil fuel) has not one oil refinery anywhere in the six-state region. A number have been proposed by foreign oil companies, by local independent oil companies, and by large American firms outside the oil industry. All of these have met with substantial opposition, largely on environmental grounds, and have been dropped. (Interestingly, no major U.S. oil company of the "Seven Sisters," the seven major oil producers, has attempted a New England refinery, instead preferring to rely on their New Jersey and Delaware refineries.) Quebec and the Maritime provinces have large, well-established oil refineries that are significantly under-utilized, with two refineries less than 100 miles from Maine in mothballs due to obsolescence, lack of product, and market. All of these eastern Canadian refineries have significant excess capacity; many are convenient to the border and the New England market; and they could readily fulfill any existing New England need for refinery capacity.

The potential benefit to New England is obvious: geographically close and economically desirable refining for the New England market, insuring product supply and economic competitiveness for the region. The benefit to Canada is also obvious: a chance to employ under-utilized facilities, to forego their possible closure, and to protect and enhance Canadian jobs. And yet, this opportunity, rational in every respect and desirable for both peoples, has been ignored. Canada has endeavored to encourage U.S. interest, but those New England groups hopeful of eventually securing a major refinery for the region have been cool to the idea of using Canadian capacity, as have been those concentrating on a justification of nuclear energy. Environmentalists, while focusing all of their attention on energy conservation and alternate forms of energy and fearful of large oil spills, have devoted little or no time to the exploration of bilateral energy opportunities (thus failing to take advantage of an opportunity to achieve their long-term goals). Washington has been uninterested in any endeavor that would increase employment in Canada at the potential expense of American workers; if the U.S. government has considered the bilateral possibilities at all, it has not had the foresight to comprehend the advantages inherent in such a relationship. Perhaps the New England congressional delegation could have swayed Washington, but it has not for reasons previously mentioned. Hence, a beneficial opportunity is being lost, a national alternative is being foreclosed, and no one can assess the loss in terms of what other mutually desirable energy arrangements might have resulted.

A further opportunity being foregone is in the area of strategic (that is, defense) and product (that is, civilian) regional oil storage. The geology of Nova Scotia and other parts of the Canadian Maritimes is such that large quantities of oil can be safely stored in the region at minimal cost. The sudden and unexpected OPEC oil embargo of 1974 and its traumatic aftermath to American consumers taught the lesson of being prepared to the

United States. A reserve supply of at least a few months duration is now perceived as a necessity if trauma and disruption are to be precluded, or at least their effects alleviated. Naturally interest developed in creating such a reserve in that region of the U.S. that has both oil and oil storage capacity: the Gulf Coast of Louisiana and its great subterranean salt domes. However, it is a long way from Louisiana to New England, and New Englanders want their product supply closer, even if it were across an international border. In fact, New England has worked diligently to secure the choice of Canada's Maritimes for the product reserve, but thus far to no avail. Louisiana's political power and the drive for energy security (in the narrowest sense, meaning a supply on—or under—U.S. soil) has prevailed; Washington has again rejected its opportunity to collaborate productively with Canada on a matter of mutual benefit.

Another aspect of oil storage is that of securing a strategic reserve for military or strategic civilian purposes in the event of an embargo's occurring during (or itself causing) a national emergency. Many of the same factors centered around the Louisiana–Maritimes competition were again at play here, only the concerns over storage on U.S. rather than foreign soil were even stronger. Once again, New England interests aligned with the Canadian position but were outmaneuvered by Washington with its southern backing. It is difficult to determine which way the national interest would have been best served; but there is no doubt that these thus far lost opportunity costs in U.S.-Canadian relations must be subtracted on the tally sheet of any historical assessment of the U.S. energy policy. Possibly these opportunities will present themselves once again at a future time; the present climate of declining energy demand, a world oil glut, world-wide surplus refining capacity, and a relationship characterized by serious energy problems is certainly not conducive now.

Canada's Energy Dilemma

The province of Ontario has significantly overbuilt its electrical generating capacity, largely with coal-fired and nuclear generating plants. Quebec is developing the enormous James Bay hydro project in the face of declining electrical demand and a limited market. New Brunswick is completing a nuclear plant and hopes to build another, with both its own needs and those of New England in mind. Manitoba is planning for significant new hydro development in the north. Saskatchewan, Alberta, and British Columbia are all rapidly developing fossil fuel and hydro reserves. The federal government in Ottawa is strongly encouraging and significantly assisting ambitious Arctic and outer continental shelf energy development, as well as the development of Alberta and Saskatchewan tar sands and heavy oils. While partly based in a concern over energy self-sufficiency and a desire to replace dependency on OPEC oil, these Canadian developments are partially a result of a desire to experience the economies of scale that are associated with large-scale development. To develop energy on such a large scale requires significant capital, often necessitating reliance on foreign sources and markets larger than those that Canada can provide. Hence, it is often American capital that helps to make these "megaprojects" possible, while these projects become increasingly dependent on American markets.

We have already seen the role of those American markets with respect to the Maritimes natural gas pipeline and Hydro Quebec's James Bay project. It is increasingly evident that New Brunswick's Point Lepreau nuclear plant will substantially serve an export function. If a second unit were built, it would largely be premised on export. (New Brunswick's Coleson Cove oil-fired plant has exported half of its electricity since its inception.) Ontario Hydro is aggressively seeking export markets from Vermont to Minnesota, at one time even seeking the opportunity to supply nonbordering New Jersey with electricity that would have been provided by the Three Mile Island nuclear plant had a famous accident not closed that plant down. (Ontario eventually lost this market to Michigan coal-fired utilities.) Manitoba is aggressively searching for markets in Nebraska and elsewhere in the American heartland, while dreaming of northern hydro development to supply this need. The western provinces hope to export more natural gas and oil on their own terms to American customers and are attending to coal and hydro possibilities as well.

Canadians have long since learned that they can build on a large scale and thus enjoy sizable economies if they build for *both* national markets simultaneously. The ideal is to overbuild at today's costs in the hope that ultimately the Canadian market will expand to absorb the excess, at which time the export component could be phased out. However, this ideal often goes unrealized because either the Canadian market does not expand rapidly enough or overbuilding occurs too soon to permit demand to catch up. The end result, whether intentional or not, is an organized effort to build for export. Politically, it is not possible in Canada to build a power-generating facility exclusively for export; but building for what are called the long-term needs of the domestic market has, in fact, sufficed to justify exports.

Another Canadian ideal often expressed but so far largely unrealized is the desire to minimize raw energy export while utilizing that energy at home, to create jobs, and to use both energy and jobs to manufacture finished goods for the export market. Lack of an export market for those products (or an economy to produce them) has been somewhat counterbalanced by a substantial export market for Canada's electricity and other raw energy. The ideal remains strong, however, among Canadian nationalists, who equate energy with the nation's birthright and thus have a strong aversion to the export of energy in any form.

There should be little question over the mutual benefit of Canadian hydroelectric generating facilities prebuilt for the U.S. market. Hydroelectricity is clean and renewable nearly forever (although its environmental impact onsite is considerable and high voltage electricity transmission is becoming an increasing source of concern). Its development at today's lesser costs would be financed by American markets and leave Canada, in the long term, with an energy supply for the future.

Although somewhat contrary to current practice, Canada can legally authorize energy supply contracts for a term of twenty-five years. The benefit to the United States is the opportunity to obtain relief from its vulnerable dependence on foreign oil for a period sufficient in length to allow development of alternative energy sources. From the Canadian viewpoint, the export of raw energy can constitute a substantial opportunity cost given the higher value of goods that could be produced domestically using that energy and thence exported. However, does Canada have that opportunity and therefore suffer that opportunity cost? The answer appears to be no, for options associated with the export, the resultant cash flow, and the economies of scale appear to be foreclosed, at least in the near term. Thus, is Canada wise to export what it can, that is, energy, for a cash return? The question is for Canadians to answer, and thus far the provinces have been enthusiastic about such exports. The federal government is a bit more reluctant, but clearly not opposed.

About 1970, numbers of U.S.-owned multinational oil companies operating in Canada were discussing ambitious plans for natural gas export to the United States. Canadian nationalism was in resurgence at that time, centered largely in the academic communities; and serious questions of selling Canada's birthright and compromising the ability of future generations to use domestic energy resources for their own purposes began to be raised. No one knew if energy export commitments made to the United States would leave Canada with enough energy for its own future needs. Nor was there any certainty concerning a fair and equitable price for the energy. The most fundamental issue centered on whether Canada could realistically hope to turn off the tap once it was opened. Canada's experience with the Columbia River Treaty, which many Canadians felt benefited the U.S. at the expense of Canada, and the opportunity cost associated with undervaluing the electricity of the Skagit–High Ross Dam to US. benefit, were fresh in mind. With the acquiescence of political leadership to this nationalistic pressure, the pace of energy export slowed, only to be speeded up again with the advent of new opportunities in electricity export in the late 1970s.

The role of such nationalism has not disappeared, however; nor is it reasonable to expect it will or should disappear, as long as the greater proportion of Canada's energy industry is controlled by U.S. interests. Canada's new National Energy Program, developed in the early 1980s and deeply resented in some American quarters, is designed to reduce foreign ownership of Canadian energy resources (in effect, oil and gas) from 80 to 90 percent to 50 percent or less by the 1990s. It is also designed to give the Canadian government a substantial role in the new Canadian component of that industry, by effectively placing one-fourth control of the northern territories' and offshore energy reserves in federal hands and by increasing federal investment, along with the provinces and private sector, in large-scale energy development in southern Canada (for example, the Alberta tar sands and heavy oils). Its mandate also expands the federal role in retailing. Canada's tendency toward government intervention and control is thus significantly displayed.

Thus is illustrated Canada's central dilemma not only in energy but in the general conduct of its economic life: accept significant foreign investment and foreign control and enjoy the jobs and other material fruits of that investment; or reject that investment and its foreign control, sacrifice the material fruits, accept the resultant hardship, but enjoy a higher level of independence (that is, home rule, self-determination). The extension of this dilemma relates to markets: Is Canada best advised to develop and thus become more or less dependent on export markets to provide the cash flow for rapid development of its resources, its economy, and its standard of living; or is the country best advised to go slowly, leave its resources undeveloped, and evolve internally at clear short-term economic sacrifice? Of course, the ideal for any nation is a mixture of the two, which calls for transforming one's own raw materials into finished products (that is, achieving as much processing as possible), then seeking export markets for those goods. This kind of growth keeps jobs at home and brings in better profits. Assuming the idea is unachievable, as it seems to be in Canada's case, a nation faces the kind of choice outlined above. Even as Canada ponders that choice, however, existing opportunities clearly beneficial to both the United States and Canada should not be overlooked.

As noted above, mutual benefits can accrue from the construction of natural gas pipelines, the development of new oil and gas fields, and the pre-building of hydroelectric facilities. The United States and Canada have also enjoyed benefits from electricity exchanges and oil swaps and are beginning to explore areas ripe for joint energy research.

International electricity exchanges between the United States and Canada have been going on since 1901. Many benefits for consumers on both sides of the border become evident when such exchanges are developed. The demand period for expensive peaking power is generally heaviest in the summer in the United States and in the winter in Canada, making the sharing of facilities for this purpose one attractive alternative. International electricity exchanges also offer the opportunity to reduce costs through the construction of larger facilities; foster cooperation between local utilities in planning, operation, and maintenance; utilize surplus energy more efficiently; and reduce dependence on oil. In 1978, over 100 transmission lines between the two countries transferred more than 8,000 megawatts of power. This capability has been projected to reach 11,000 megawatts by the mid-1980s.

Swapping oil supplies along the long border has provided a means for each country to avoid the high transportation costs of shipping their domestic oil supplies to areas where the other country has supplies more readily available. The ability to transfer both oil and electricity provides a short-term security to the peoples of both countries against any disruption of service.

If technology were to permit, the United States and Canada could answer all future energy needs with their rich coal reserves. Considerable opportunities exist to increase joint research and development in coal technology for liquefaction and gasification, fluidized bed combustion, coal-in-oil combustion, and environmental controls. Every joint success in advanced coal technology would tend to strengthen the security of North America against energy vulnerability and bring closer a day of energy independence.

Similarly, the province of Alberta has oil deposits locked in deep tar sands equal in amount to those of Saudi Arabia. The United States entered into a modest joint demonstration project for the extraction of this massive energy source, but the surface is barely scratched. Conversely, vast U.S. resources of oil shale in Colorado, Wyoming, and Utah could benefit both peoples.

The transnational area, with both the market and the natural resources, that offers the greatest opportunity for cooperation on a major scale, now and for the remainder of this century, is the Eastern Canadian provinces and the northeastern United States. This region has a long history of cooperative interaction, as well as a shared geography, population, and heritage that have made north-south trade routes a fact of life there. By market standards and by population, Atlantic Canada, with a population of under 2 million, is small when compared to the northeastern United States and its population of 40 million located in an energy-demanding industrial region. However, the New England states are an energy-starved area, suffering from high prices and periodic short supplies, particularly as a result of dependence on imported oil for 70 percent of their energy needs.

New England is an attractive market for natural gas, which currently accounts for only 9 percent of its energy mix, compared to 25 percent nationwide. The New England market for electricity is equally strong, amounting to over 6 billion dollars in the early 1980s. Nuclear power plants have not proved to be the answer to New England's need. By the turn of the century, the Nuclear Regulatory Commission licenses for all four of the nuclear plants now operating in New England will have expired, making their continued future questionable.

The vast amounts of natural gas and hydro capacity that characterize Canada west of New Brunswick create an energy surplus in central Canada and leave little immediate need for additional output of the magnitude now being planned in the Atlantic Provinces. Some of those energy development plans now under way in the Atlantic provinces are of megaproportions and can find natural markets only in the northeastern United States.

For example, in 1982 one oil company executive, discussing a discovery of 9 trillion cubic feet of gas and recoverable oil reserves of 2 billion barrels, estimated that this amounted to only 15 percent of the potential existing in the 3,500-square-mile area between the Baffin Strait and the Scotian Shelf. Expressing renewed interest in the harnessing of the giant tides of the Bay of Fundy, Nova Scotia has created North America's first tidal-power–generating station as a pilot study for further development. The province has plans to move to the first stage of construction of a 6,000-megawatt facility.

In addition, Hydro Quebec's plans for future developments, the exploitation of Labrador's Lower Churchill Falls, New Brunswick power company exports, construction of new gas pipelines, new electrical transmission lines, and increased coal extraction in Nova Scotia all hold promise for the creation of economic activity in the northeastern United States–Quebec–Atlantic Canada international region not experienced since the region's earliest beginnings.

The opportunity for greater cooperation in energy matters is available now. In the final analysis, whether such a course is undertaken will depend on the attitudes of the two peoples and the questions they ask. They will have to decide whether to make choices on the basis of what is best for their individual countries or, in contrast, on the basis of what is best for North America. If the latter is chosen, then Canada, as the smaller of the two nations, must determine if it can protect its identity and growth within that context. This is a concern of all North Americans, for a stronger, stable, and self-confident Canada would be of inestimable value to the United States and to the western world. Future bilateral economic policy, and particularly the energy component of that policy, will play a central role in this choice of attitudes.

For its part the United States should avoid terms such as "continental oil policy," that carry one-sided connotations and place its considerable muscle behind those energy opportunities that are clearly mutually beneficial—not only for the United States and Canada but for the many deprived areas of the world.

Notes

1. The economic realities of the early 1980s, with general oil and energy surplus, decreasing demand for electricity and other energy forms, and high interest rates and economic recession, all reduce the opportunities described

in this chapter; and they especially inhibit the development of large, capital-intensive energy projects. Whether this condition signifies a fundamental change in western industrial society, or whether it constitutes an aberrant "blip" on the longer-term horizon, we cannot know at this time, though most industry analysts believe the latter to be the case.

2. See John E. Carroll, "Energy and the Northeast: The Canadian Connection," *Energy Policy and Public Administration,* ed. G. Daneke and F. Lagassa (D.C. Heath & Co., Boston, 1980), chap. 18.

6

Formalizing the Relationship: The Case of the International Joint Commission

The diplomatic relationship between the United States and Canada is for the most part an ad hoc relationship, one that is characterized by a minimum of formal principles, rules of procedure, or institutions to carry them out. This characterization is valid in spite of the great complexity and intensity of the relationship.

There are, however, a few institutions and their associated formalized procedures that are important in certain narrow aspects of the diplomatic relationship, such as the Great Lakes Fisheries Commission, the Permanent Joint Board on Defense, the Canada-U.S. Ministerial Committee on Trade and Economic Affairs (now inactive), and, among the most important, the International Joint Commission (IJC). Because the IJC has been active a long time (nearly three-quarters of a century), because it has been looked to as a model of bilateral institutionalization by the world's nations, because it has successfully tackled a number of major tasks, and because it is unique in its own right, there is good reason to consider the IJC as an institutional case study in this volume.[1] To the degree that the concept behind the commission begins to spawn new ideas relevant to the governance of the future bilateral relationship, attention to the IJC at this time is doubly rewarding.

The Boundary Waters Treaty and the Commission

Bilateral demand for international boundary water for irrigation in the prairies and for Great Lakes water for hydroelectricity at Niagara Falls had become so competitive by the turn of the century that it was evident that a treaty or some other type of diplomatic arrangement to fairly allocate these increasingly valuable waters would soon be needed. Serious pollution problems in parts of the Great Lakes and their connecting channels were also becoming evident. A number of bilateral environmental issues were coalescing, such as the drive to establish a St. Lawrence Seaway for navigation; the unilateral (U.S.) construction of the Chicago Diversion Canal; the St. Mary River–Milk River irrigation dispute on the western prairies; hydroproject proposals for the St. Mary's River at Sault Ste. Marie, Michigan, and Ontario, which required bilateral action; concern over protection of Niagara Falls and interest in hydroelectricity diversions from the falls; and a proposed damming of the outlet of Lake Erie. All these projects supported the need for concerted joint bilateral action.

It was the matter of irrigation on the western prairies and a Montana–Alberta conflict over water allocation, coupled with a joint interest in establishing an international commission to investigate the conditions and uses of water in the Great Lakes–St. Lawrence system, that culminated in the first institutional action, the establishment in 1905 of the weak but symbolically significant International Waterways Commission (IWC). The main value of the IWC was as a platform to advance ideas on bilateral boundary water relations and as an access route to the top levels of government. The IWC, though purely advisory, is credited with developing the concepts of equitable distribution of water between the two countries and of navigation as paramount to all other water uses after domestic supply. These concepts were accepted by both countries. The commission is also credited with extending its jurisdiction beyond the Great Lakes–St. Lawrence system to encompass all boundary waters. With the general bilateral acceptance of these and a few other basic tenets, including prohibition of the diversion of streams crossing the boundary as well as of pollution in one country that would cause injury in the other, the foundation was laid and serious negotiation of a treaty could begin. That negotiation would lead to the signing of the Boundary Waters Treaty of 1909 and the establishment of the International Joint Commission.

The smaller of the two nations, Canada (then represented by the United Kingdom in foreign relations) opted for a strong treaty with strong methods of implementation, a natural position for the smaller power, which gains from any formula equalizing sovereign powers. The United States, the larger of the two, ever protective of its sovereignty, and jealous of perceived assaults thereon, opted for a weaker treaty and implementation vehicle because it did not want its power compromised.

The Canadian negotiators wanted essentially a supranational institution that would be given charge of all boundary and cross-boundary matters. U.S. negotiators argued that the treaty draft departed from the established practice of the U.S. government to avoid submitting questions not already at issue to an international tribunal, that it empowered the commission to deal with matters otherwise under the undisputed control of the U.S. government, and that the commission might ultimately create international law. The result of this debate was compromise: the United States softened its stand on the commission's scope and authority but won a Canadian concession for its view that waters that did not actually straddle the boundary should be excluded, and that arbitration in the case of deadlock should not be automatic.

Canada's initiative toward a strong treaty led to the creation of an independent body called the International Joint Commission with absolute and unappealable powers in certain limited areas of water allocation at the border. U.S. opposition led to the placing of strict limits on this power, and also to restriction of the commission to an advisory role in all other areas, including most importantly water quality (and, more recently, air quality) matters. Because the two federal governments make all IJC appointments and because they control the flow of most work to the commission, it can be said that the commission (and hence the treaty) is as strong or as weak as the two governments wish it to be at any one point in time.

What was needed and created was a permanent method of direct contact between Ottawa and Washington, principled, beyond local prejudice and interest, and without national bias. And while the concept that ultimately led to the establishment of the IJC was a central part of the treaty negotiation, the treaty also set out to establish the future rules by which the boundary waters relationship would be governed and to settle other differences. The principal purpose of the Boundary Waters Treaty of 1909 was to create joint machinery that could

> ...prevent disputes regarding the use of boundary waters and to settle all questions which are now pending between the United States and the Dominion of Canada involving the rights, obligations or interests of either in relation to the other, along the common frontier, and to make provision for the adjustment and settlement of all such questions as may hereafter arise....[2]

The joint machinery is, of course, the IJC and its rules of procedure.

The treaty deals with five categories of waters:

1. boundary waters—defined as those along which the international boundary runs, and including all bays and inlets of these waters, but excluding tributaries to and distributaries from these waters;
2. upstream transboundary waters—waters that are upstream from and flow across the boundary;
3. waters that are tributary to boundary waters;
4. waters that flow from boundary waters;
5. downstream transboundary waters—waters that are downstream from the boundary, having flowed across the boundary.

The treaty's objectives were to settle all pending disputes along the frontier, and to prevent or to provide for the adjustment and settlement of similar difficulties in the future. To achieve this purpose, articles I, II, III, IV, and VIII set forth the principles that were to govern the use, obstruction, and diversion of "boundary" and transboundary waters. Article VII provided for the creation of the Joint Commission, and individual articles listed the four categories of functions that the new agency was expected to discharge. These articles are administrative (article VI, which directs the measurement and division of the waters of the Milk and St. Mary rivers); quasi-judicial (articles III, IV, and VIII, which allow for the passing upon of applications for permission to use, divert, or obstruct treaty waters); arbitral (article X, which provides for binding decisions relative to *any* questions arising between the two countries); and investigative (article IX, which provides for examining and making recommendations on any difference arising along the common boundary).[3]

The International Joint Commission was established under the Boundary Waters Treaty to administer and discharge the purposes of the treaty. The commission is composed of three Canadian members who are appointed by the governor in council (prime minister and Cabinet) for terms, and three U.S. members who are appointed by the president with Senate approval and who serve at the president's pleasure. Each section, Canadian and American, has a full-time chairman, with the other commissioners serving part-time. Each section is served by a small full-time staff of professionals in Ottawa and Washington. These staffs include experts trained in a range of disciplines from the traditional engineering and law to the more recent addition of economics and biology. The commission also administers the Great Lakes Water Quality Agreements of 1972 and 1978.

The real work of the commission, however, is carried out by the various boards and groups (investigative boards, pollution surveillance boards, boards of control, Water Quality Board, Science Advisory Board, and two reference groups—Upper Lakes and Pollution from Land Use). These bodies are composed of career civil servants, mainly engineers and various scientists, who are "seconded" (that is, borrowed) from a number of federal agencies, commonly including Environment Canada (especially the Inland Waters Directorate), Environmental Protection Agency, U.S. Army Corps of Engineers, U.S. Bureau of Reclamation, and the U.S. Geological Survey. These boards and groups provide formal reports and recommendations to the six commissioners who, in turn, refer this output to their Washington and Ottawa professional staffs for further refinement, prior to determining their own final recommendations and advice. (The two reference groups, the Science Advisory Board, and the Water Quality Board are limited to work under the Great Lakes Water Quality Agreement and supplement the Great Lakes Regional Office staff at Windsor, Ontario, in advising the commission.)

Each board and its supplementary working committees are composed of an equal number of nationals of each country and serve under a co-chairman from each. The boards themselves are appointed by the commission after consultation with the government and report directly to the commission, not to their governments or their agencies. This system of seconding career bureaucrats has the advantage of obtaining for the commission some of the best expertise available and at a less direct cost (the cost being borne by their agencies rather than by the commission). It also has the advantage of leading to greater acceptability by the officials of the agencies represented and therefore by their respective governments. However, there are also disadvantages to this system. The investigative studies often take a long time to complete since those doing the work are part-time, owing a large share of their energy to their respective agencies.

The two sections of the commission, Washington and Ottawa, operate as a single unit and also as a response unit to the two governments and to the governmental and nongovernmental applicants. The commission cannot initiate its own work and thus is sharply constrained as to what it can accomplish, even though the ways in which it *could* be used are very broad indeed.

Since its creation, the commission has concentrated on five major subjects:

1. approval of hydroelectric, flood control, and reclamation and irrigation storage structures that entail flood damage upstream across the frontier;
2. approval of hydroelectric structures and navigation improvements on boundary waters;
3. application for approval of assorted minor river works;
4. water appropriations from boundary and transboundary waters, both intra- and inter-basin;
5. investigations of various types (for example, lake levels and Great Lakes water pollution).

The IJC essentially has two broad categories of authority, judicial and investigative. The right to approve or reject applications for projects affecting boundary waters, waters flowing from boundary waters, and transboundary waters below the boundary constitute the commission's judicial authority. This can be considered compulsory jurisdiction granted under articles III and IV. The commission's binding decisions in these cases are called orders of approval and are not subject to appeal. Most of the first half century's work was of this type.

The IJC also has a broad investigative power granted under articles IX and X. Article IX confers the power to investigate, study, report and recommend, but only in an advisory sense. The IJC's findings under this article are not binding. Article X, which is yet to be used, provides for binding arbitration in *any* matter given to it by the governments. Its investigative powers can be broad, but their terms are dictated by the specific requests of either country.

The remaining specific directive given to the commission by the treaty is the order of preference of water uses to be observed in determining whether to approve an application. Uses for domestic and sanitary purposes are to be considered first, followed by navigation, power, and irrigation, in that order. This reflects a priority system that was natural in the early twentieth century but which does not represent contemporary concerns for recreational values, aesthetics, or general pollution problems; nor does it give electric power generation the high place it might well be given today.

During its first thirty years, the commission's agenda was dominated by applications for water apportionment permits, and the commission was naturally staffed mainly with engineering expertise. However, the past three decades or so have witnessed dramatic changes. As many of the old disputes were adjudicated, the commission was gradually working itself out of a job (except for the monitoring and surveillance role, which was never-ending). Simultaneously, sufficient new problems arose in the transborder water and air relationship that the two governments began to increase their requests to the commission to pass recommendations under the reference or investigative authority granted under article IX. Questions of water and air quality were arising and were increasingly referred to the commission, not for adjudication but for advice and recommendation. These questions required the expertise of lawyers, economists, and many different types of natural and physical scientists in addition to engineers. They were also often national or megaregional in scope, affecting many people, and had broad policy implications of a controversial nature. No longer could the commission quietly pronounce upon narrow technical questions of minor impact about which few knew and fewer cared. It was suddenly thrust into the public spotlight and became a very different institution with a very different role to play, in spite of no change being formalized in its powers or mandate.

The commission's new role, to tackle pollution in both water and air and to interest itself in much more abstract quality as well as quantity questions, was founded upon the original language of article IV of the Boundary Waters Treaty: "... boundary waters and waters flowing across the boundary shall not be polluted on either side to the injury of health or property on the other."[4] These are surprising words for 1909 but do represent an early mandate, upon which most current water quality and some current air quality involvement is based.

Former Canadian Section Chairman Maxwell Cohen views the commission as having gone through four distinct stages:

a. the period of shaping the work of the Commission, from 1912 to the beginning of World War II ...;
b. the "great works" period of post–World War II (a reference to the St. Lawrence Power and Seaway and Columbia River issues);
c. the gradual shift away from Orders of Approval to References after 1956 as the principal work of the Commission ...;
d. the growing importance of air pollution and water quality problems and the emergence of an increasingly environmental perspective from 1960 onwards ....[5]

As Cohen has concluded, the fundamental importance of the commission itself

> ... is the notion of its unity, of its "singleness" in operation, of its independence from both Governments, of the binding character of its Orders of

Approval on both Governments, and the fact that it can carry out, as it deems fit, the interpretive and quasi-judicial process required of it.[6]

It is often said that the treaty and the commission have failed to come close to achieving their potential. One reason for the truth of this statement is the enormous gap between what the commission has accomplished and what in fact it could accomplish if encouraged by the two federal governments.

First, there is literally no limit to the kind of work that can be requested from the commission in the bilateral sphere. It is not limited to boundary waters or environmental questions—it could be used in such unrelated areas as energy, trade, and even bilateral cultural disputes. The commission's tradition and expertise, however, is in environmental sciences; and it could not be useful in other areas without significant change in its nature.

Second, the commission through article X of the Boundary Waters Treaty does have the power of binding arbitration, again in virtually any bilateral area. Yet, in spite of its long history and the many disputes that have called for such a binding arbitral presence, the article has never been invoked. The commission must await federal invocation of the article by Ottawa and Washington—and such has never been forthcoming.

A third area of lost opportunity has been the failure to use the commission in the marine environment or in the Arctic. These environments have witnessed bilateral disputes (such as over pollution and fisheries) that could have and still could benefit from IJC expertise. The inland freshwater tradition, though, continues to dominate the agenda. (Minor IJC involvement in the Passamaquoddy tidal project and the Point Roberts dispute stand as minute exceptions of marine involvement.)

Finally, the federal governments have been criticized for failure to respond to continual IJC warnings of developing problems—an especially valid criticism in the air quality area; failure to utilize the commission to tackle the serious acid rain issue (concerning which, in fact, the commission deserves credit for forewarning the two governments concerning the inherent bilateral dangers); for failure to respond to many of the commission's recommendations in recent years (with the Garrison issue being a prime example); for over-politicizing appointments to the commission or, during the past few years, for permitting vacancies on the commission to remain for long periods. This litany of criticism could continue; but the point being made is that, for all their rhetoric about the uniqueness and high value of the treaty and the International Joint Commission, the two federal governments have not strongly supported the implementation of the treaty and are directly responsible for any gap between the IJC's performance and potential.

A Need for Change

As has been noted, much has changed since the IJC was created in 1909. While the concept of the IJC has been proven and its validity increased over the years, in a structural and operational sense it has not kept pace with that change. This became painfully obvious to the senior author of this book during his tenure as a U.S. member of the Commission.[7]

The more deliberative operating style of earlier years has become inadequate to meet current workloads. It is not unusual for a report to the governments to now take two to three years to complete from receipt of the reference. This inability to meet current demands has two serious effects upon the commission, namely, the report may lose its value or governments may hesitate to utilize the commission on new matters.

The reference on the water quality of the Poplar River in Saskatchewan is a case in point. The IJC was requested in August, 1977, to study the transboundary water quality implications of the development of a thermal power plant by the Saskatchewan Power Corporation. The plant was under construction just a few miles from the Montana border. Although the IJC ultimately submitted an interim report to the governments in March of 1979, the ensuing problems were solved through bilateral negotiations prior to and without the benefit of the IJC's final report.[8]

Such delays are caused in part because the commission still functions with four of the six commissioners working on a part-time basis, while the commission has been organized in a fashion that requires the involvement of all six of its members. During the senior author's tenure on the commission, few of the administrative matters were delegated by the full-time chairmen, and these time-consuming mechanical tasks were thus still being directed by the commissioners themselves rather than by their highly competent technical staffs or seconded bureaucrats. The many important but burdensome public hearings were still demanding the attendance of all commissioners and several staff members to take the testimony from public witnesses, who often were fewer than three in number. The appointment of full-time commissioners and the institution of modernized operational techniques would correct many of the commission's administrative shortcomings.

More troublesome, however, is the commission's dependency upon the international boards for the development of technical information. Board members with full-time, high-level positions within other governmental agencies are already functioning on limited budgets, staff, and time, which affects the timeliness of the IJC response. It is also difficult at times to expect board members to supply technical advice that could result in a conflict with their primary responsibility. But, in the final analysis, the work of the international boards is highly professional and is performed at substantial savings to both governments.

The IJC commissioners function in a remarkably impartial manner with a minimum of nationalistic concerns. Reforms to the commission are necessary, not as a criticism of its past performance, but as a means of more fully utilizing its potential.

Possible Reforms

Aside from reform in the thinking and attitude of the two federal governments toward the commission and a greater willingness to surrender that portion of national sovereignty necessary to enable the treaty to truly serve the national interest of both nations, as it was meant to do, there are some specific reforms in the IJC process that might well enable it to serve the governments better.[9] All such reforms have their advantages and disadvantages, but there are many that are worthy of serious trial.

Critics of the IJC often like to focus on what they see as a fundamental legal weakness—the omission of provisions that would have made it the strong arbitral body that its British progenitors envisaged. In retrospect, this omission is desirable; without question, fewer references (that is, directives from the two federal governments which seek nonbinding advice and recommendations) would be given over to IJC dominion if either government knew it had no recourse under the law but to accept IJC decisions as final judgments. Such power would undoubtedly be regarded as an attack on national sovereignty and could lead ultimately to the demise of the IJC. It is in the best interests of both nations for the two governments and their respective foreign offices, the Department of State and the Department of External Affairs, to retain basic negotiating leverage and final authority in the issues referred to the IJC.

On the other hand, the critics' concerns about the IJC's legal responsibility for references are more justified. Not only is the commission left out of certain critical categories of transboundary environmental problems, such as marine pollution and Arctic environmental quality, but the commission is also constrained by the deliberately narrow wording of references that precludes it from investigating problem areas bearing on the central reference. For example, it appears impossible on the Poplar River issue to separate water quality from water quantity. Yet the IJC had to do just that from 1974, the year of the water diversion reference, to late 1977, when the water quality reference was finally issued. Because quantity and quality are so closely related, most water resource specialists agree that the two cannot be studied separately (especially in smaller basins).

Traditional bureaucratic cross-currents run between the IJC, the U.S. State Department, and the Canadian Department of External Affairs. On the one hand, IJC commissioners at times seek to reach beyond their roles as currently mandated by their respective governments. On the other hand, the personnel assigned by the State Department and External Affairs sometimes give the appearance of attempting to direct the commission, and more often leave the impression that it would be preferable to negotiate through existing diplomatic channels without any commission involvement. Indeed, a much needed reform involves giving the IJC initiatory powers: the power to undertake its own references as it sees fit, within established but broad guidelines, and with the approval of the respective governments.

Professor Maxwell Cohen, former chairman of the Canadian section of the IJC, has recently alluded to this need: "... the Commission may have to have the capability of undertaking its own preliminary inquiries wherever its emerging environmental-developmental perspectives alert it to possible difficult issues arising along the common frontier."[10] Others have also recommended that initiatory authority to request references (that is, the power to initiate its own work) be granted to the commission. Given such authority, many serious disputes could well be avoided. This change and such other reforms as the power to publicize its findings (now granted only on Great Lakes' water quality issues) are needed if the commission is to realize its effective potential. Yet it would not be desirable to renegotiate the treaty itself to accomplish such ends. Professor Cohen summarized the feeling of many Canadian officials when he wrote that "[t]he Boundary Waters Treaty is flexible enough to allow for creative interpretation in the future. Ironically, in the present Canadian–United States mood, the Treaty probably could not be even drafted today, to say nothing of being agreed upon by both countries."[11] Reform must be achieved without going through negotiation processes that would involve federal-provincial relations in Canada. Professor Cohen, a respected authority on Canada's international legal arrangements, believes this is possible.

The need for IJC reform is not restricted to the powers of the commission; the structure and staffing of the commission itself, particularly in the United States section, needs examination. The successful effort of Senator Gaylord Nelson of Wisconsin to pass an amendment that requires Senate approval of the president's nominees to the commission is a step in the right direction. Although the U.S. Senate Committee on Foreign Relations as well as the full Senate regard this duty as one of very low priority, it may have the effect of encouraging the president to exercise more care in selecting nominees in the future, as well as providing the all-important signal of presidential interest.

The first reform should be a separation of the IJC's annual budget appropriation from the overall State Department budget, where it now appears as a line item. This removal is necessary if complete separation is to be maintained between the commission and the bilateral agency, as intended in the treaty. A second improvement would be direct funding for the IJC, at least on a trial basis, so that other government agencies do not have to bear its costs indirectly. A third would be the mandating of equal funding of the IJC by both governments. Currently, the Canadian section is better funded and has a higher manpower allocation. There is a need for significant increase in the U.S. budgetary commitment to the IJC. A fourth reform would create full-time commissioners. At present, only the chairmen are full time; and the complexity of current problems demands full-time attention by all six commissioners. A fifth requirement would give all commissioners specific terms of office, with terms staggered to ensure no more than a one-third turnover at any one time. Only Canadian commissioners have terms now, while United States commissioners serve at the pleasure of the president.

A final reform pertains to the composition of the technical boards and various other IJC boards of inquiry that assist the commission in making its recommendations. These boards have been composed almost exclusively of federal and, less frequently, state and provincial bureaucrats, who more often than not have engineering backgrounds. The composition of these boards must be broadened, a transformation that has started with the appointment of biologists, economists, geologists, soil scientists, and an occasional social scientist. However, the pace is too slow and the proportion less than sufficient. A second reform in board composition involves the almost total dominance there by government officials. While officials from federal, state, and provincial governments have a place as long as their professional expertise is required, their numbers should be reduced. Greater participation by the public, academics, private businessmen, citizen leaders, and others should balance both the approaches and the views of the boards. This inclusion would be more expensive, at least on paper, than the present system of seconding federal bureaucrats; but the costs of the present system are heavy. Seconded bureaucrats cannot perform well at their own agencies if they are working for the IJC. There is the additional cost to society of their supporting narrow, unbalanced, and less than ideal decisions. No matter how hard they try, these bureaucrats cannot be something other than what they are—veteran employees of government agencies who must, by definition, reflect the ways of doing business, if not the views themselves, of the agencies from which they are seconded. Hence, the approaches, methods, and views of Canada's Inland Waters Directorate and the United States Army Corps of Engineers, Bureau of Reclamation and Geological Survey dominate all IJC boards, as these agencies are the sources of a large percentage of current board membership. In proper proportion, these approaches have their value; but they must be balanced by the intelligence and creativity that the nongovernmental sectors of our societies are willing to contribute.

Reform is also needed in the IJC's relations with the public, in both a formal structural sense and in an informal communications-education sense. In terms of formal structure, one possibility is the establishment of an appointed citizens' advisory committee that can make direct input to the IJC. This group would be similar to the IJC Science Advisory Board on the Great Lakes, but would work in all areas of IJC responsibility. Such a committee would be composed of representatives of citizens' groups, academics, and perhaps the business community. The prevailing membership should have environmental credentials, but to achieve balance it should also include a few experts on U.S.-Canadian relations. While a regional balance should also be sought, qualifications should be deemed to be more important. In addition, the Canadian Senate's Standing Committee on Foreign Affairs has recommended that the commission should also have extended power to publicize all its recommendations. The IJC should be given the funds to publish a monthly newsletter and a more extensive in-depth quarterly journal featuring analysis by both the IJC and external opinion.

Four additional reforms could enable the IJC to realize its potential. The first is a complete and total separation from the departments of State and External Affairs. The Canadian section's decision to turn down office space in the Lester B. Pearson Building (the headquarters of External Affairs in Ottawa) was a step in the right direction; but greater procedural separation, particularly in Washington, is needed. A second reform is a physical location that would permit maximum integration of the two sections and staffs. Preliminary discussions on exchange or rotation of staff between Ottawa and Washington are a small step in this direction; but attention should also be given to locating the whole commission in one building, perhaps in a near-border city such as Minneapolis or Winnipeg, near the middle of the continent. Another need is to avoid the domination of the Great Lakes Water Quality Agreements over other issues. So much attention and funding have been devoted to them that all other issues could be swamped. A final desirable reform is an expansion of involvement in air quality. The IJC should develop significant expertise and with it a public reputation in the air quality and acid precipitation areas, subjects that are taking up more and more of the commission's time. Concurrently it should be assigned major responsibility for refining and carrying out policy developed under the U.S.-Canadian air quality agreements now in early negotiation.

The gap between the International Joint Commission in theory and in rhetoric on the one hand, and the International Joint Commission in practice and in reality on the other, is an enormous one. The commission stands as a tangible example of the fact that for all the good feeling that exists between the two nations, the will to surrender sovereignty for the common good is lacking. Until this spirit of compromise can be developed, the IJC, for all of its promise, will function significantly below potential.

Notes

1. Some of the material in this chapter is modified from John E. Carroll, *Environmental Diplomacy* (University of Michigan Press, Ann Arbor, Michigan, 1983), and also is taken from John E. Carroll, "Patterns Old and New," in R. Spencer, J. Kirton, and K. Nossal, *The International Joint Commission Seventy Years On* (Toronto: University of Toronto Center for International Studies, 1981).

2. Treaty between the United States and Great Britain relating to boundary waters and questions arising between the United States and Canada, January 11, 1909, *Canada Statutes,* 1911, chap. 28, art. 7.

3. See William Willoughby, *The Joint Organizations of Canada and the United States* (University of Toronto Press, 1979).

4. International Joint Commission, *Rules of Procedure and Text of Treaty,* p. 14.

5. Maxwell Cohen, "Canada and the United States: Dispute Settlement and the International Joint Commission—Can This Experience be Applied to Law of the Sea Issues?" *Journal of International Law,* 8 (Winter 1976):77. Reprinted with permission.

6. Maxwell Cohen, "The Hague Lectures," (The Hague Academy, 1975), p. 257. Reprinted with permission.

7. Kenneth M. Curtis was a member of the U.S. Section of the International Joint Commission, 1978–1979.

8. For further detail on the Poplar Power Plant Issue, see John E. Carroll, *Environmental Diplomacy* (1983).

9. See Carroll, "Patterns Old and New."

10. Maxwell Cohen, "Canada and the United States," p. 79.

11. Ibid.

7 Special Relationships between States and Provinces

Canada and the United States stretch some 3,500 miles from the Atlantic to the Pacific oceans through areas of varying climates, resources, and geography. Thus the concerns and livelihood of the Canadian and American people living along the border are often more similar on a bi-national regional basis, a north-south basis, rather than on an east-west basis within their respective countries. Given the fact that over three-fourths of Canada's 24 million people live within 100 miles of the border, and given the location along that border of many municipalities that could easily be called "international sister cities," the pull of the north-south regional orientation of the U.S.-Canadian relationship becomes more understandable. The interaction of the northern U.S. Plains states and the Canadian Prairie provinces, the New England states and Quebec and the Maritimes, the U.S. Midwest and Ontario, the U.S. Pacific Northwest and British Columbia are all indicative of such regional "pulls." Add to this scenario the extensive existing private relationships detailed in chapter 8 (that is, existing family and economic ties), and it becomes evident why people with common concerns and access to easy communication do not always wait for the cumbersome machinery of diplomacy to work. This informality is one reason why several relationships have developed between subnational levels of the U.S. and Canadian governments.[1]

The Canadian Senate's Standing Committee on Foreign Affairs, studying the institutional framework of U.S.-Canadian relations, analyzed direct province-state contacts and found that such contacts fall into a number of categories: meetings of a "mini-summit" nature between premiers and governors, most often of neighboring provinces and states (for example, New England governors–Eastern Canadian premiers, Washington–British Columbia–Yukon–Alaska, and Michigan–Ontario); informal but official contacts between state and provincial officials representing mutual areas of concern (such as transportation, public safety, environment, and agriculture); and conferences of provincial and state legislators designed to enhance cooperation or resolve mutual problems.[2]

Prior to 1974, little knowledge had been collected to define the extent of these subnational-level interactions. Dr. Roger Swanson's 1974 study, *State-Province Interaction,* revealed an extensive number of informal "agreements, arrangements, and understandings."[3] Swanson discovered that the largest number of interactions (211 of the 766 reported) involved public transportation (for example, highways, vehicle licenses, and insurance). The second most active subject was natural resources, with 149 total interactions. Other interests receiving considerable attention were agriculture, commerce and industry, education and culture, energy, environmental protection, human services, military and civil defense, and public safety. All fifty states were involved with formal interactions with the ten Canadian provinces, but the border states were understandably the most active, with the state of Maine alone accounting for 110 of those interactions. The Organization for Economic Cooperation and Development (OECD) has compiled a summary list of such transnational regional linkages in North America (see table 7-1).

The Case of Maine

A closer examination of the Maine experience provides practical case examples of a wide variety of interactions with more than a single province and the techniques that have been employed to carry them out. The state of Maine, sharing two-thirds of its land boundary with two Canadian provinces (Quebec and New Brunswick) and having nearly 20 percent of its population of Canadian descent, typifies the subnational (and also the private) relationship existing between the Canadian and American peoples. Quebec and Maine share in the rich French-speaking heritage of North America, while Maine and the Maritime provinces of New Brunswick, Nova Scotia, and, to a lesser degree, Prince Edward Island, are dependent upon similar resources and experience many of the same economic benefits and difficulties that have historically affected the region. These factors make cooperative development and problem solving an appealing way of getting the job done and at the same time of stretching insufficient financial resources.

In the early 1970s, Maine entered into dialogues individually with Quebec, New Brunswick, Nova Scotia, and also collectively with the Eastern Canadian provinces. This activity soon became so intense that, in 1973, Maine became the first state in the nation to establish a State Office of Canadian Relations that had as its purpose the coordination of these programs.

The most active relationship grew between Maine and New Brunswick: by 1975, 29 separate state-provincial arrangements or agreements had been reached. This effort had begun in June, 1971, with a meeting between the senior author, who was then Maine's governor, and the premier of New Brunswick, Richard Hatfield, at the U.S.-Canadian International Park on Campobello Island, New Brunswick, to discuss common problems.

A committee of state and provincial officials was established "to determine areas where cooperative programs might be mutually advantageous to both the state and the province."[4] At a second meeting that year, the governor and premier heard the report of the committee and "agreed to initiate a program of sustained cooperation in environmental, energy, trade, tourism and transportation matters."[5] Subsequently, the agreement was extended to include forestry, fisheries, recreation, and agriculture. On June 28, 1973, these meetings culminated in the signing of an agreement between the state of Maine and the province of New Brunswick. The governor and premier found that

> Actions to date in the furtherance of closer ties between Maine and New Brunswick and, in particular, the program of cooperation now existing between Maine and New Brunswick have been mutually beneficial by opening avenues of communication, by stimulating exchanges of information, material, personnel, and ideas, and by producing an increased awareness among both governmental officials and others that each has a vital interest in what transpires in the other's domain and an equally vital interest in working in close harmony with the other in a wide range of concerns.[6]

They then went on to agree as follows:

> We shall endeavor, in our respective capacities as Premier and Governor, to maintain and foster close cooperation in all relevant areas of concern consistent with such Canadian and United States federal policies as may apply and, in particular, we designate the areas of environment, energy, trade, tourism, transportation, forestry, recreation, fisheries, and agriculture as appropriate for continued and expanded common effort among agencies of Maine and New Brunswick, while acknowledging that other areas of mutually beneficial cooperation may emerge from time to time.[7]

Well-intentioned initiatives have a habit of remaining dormant but, in this instance, considerable activity transpired and real accomplishments did take place. The following are a few examples: a mutual aid agreement on civil defense that implemented the original intent of an earlier exchange of notes between the United States and Canada regarding mutual aid in civil defense; an agreement between the state and province to keep each other fully informed of civil defense resources and to make these resources available to combat any major disaster (military, civilian, natural); an agreement to institute a broad-based program of cooperation on growing concern over pollution problems; an agreement for medical, police, and fire cooperation; informal agreements on maintenance of border bridges; reciprocity in motor truck regulations and restrictions (such as weight and size); a joint program of early potato disease detection; joint research to combat the spruce budworm in the forests; and a border survey to enhance joint tourism opportunities.

The Quebec–Maine intergovernmental relationship started with two exchange visits and conferences of French-speaking legislative and executive personnel. In June, 1973, a three-day conference was held and a letter of

Table 7-1
Regional and Local Environmental, Water, and Forestry Agreements and Arrangements between Communities or Other Official Bodies in the United States and Canada

Parties	Countries	Date	Type/Purpose	Commission/Working Party
North Dakota, Montana, Minnesota Alberta, Manitoba, Saskatchewan	United States Canada		Arrangement on International Technical Information	Exchange meetings on environmental matters (Great Plains–Prairies Provinces Regions)
Montana, Alberta	United States Canada		Exchange of information on environmental matters	
Maine, New Brunswick	United States Canada	1975	Environment, forest, fishing, etc.	
Alaska, Montana, Oregon, Washington, Canadian Province (B.C.)	United States Canada		Arrangement on the Pacific North West pollution control	
Maine, New Brunswick	United States Canada	20/10/71	Arrangement to institute a broad-based program of co-operation on pollution	
Michigan, Ontario	United States Canada	1971 and 1974	Arrangement to develop an integrated co-operative air pollution control program in the Michigan–Ontario International Area	Joint hearings and common program of air pollution control (Windsor, Detroit, Sarnia, Port Huron)
New York, Ontario	United States Canada		Arrangement to discuss mutual air pollution problems	
Wisconsin, Ontario	United States Canada		Arrangements Concerning water quality	
Michigan, Ontario	United States Canada	13/6/67	Arrangement for joint policy on oil and gas drillings in Lake Huron, St. Clair River, Lake St. Clair, and Detroit River (pollution)	
Washington, British Columbia	United States Canada	10/7/72	Memorandum of understanding on oil pollution	

City of Neche (North Dakota), Water Supply, Manitoba	United States Canada	1/1/70	Agreement for the supply of drinking water to towns in Manitoba (Gretna and Altona) (240,000 gal/day for 10 years)
North Dakota Canadian towns	United States Canada		Construction of drainage facilities in Canada by an American agency
City of Seattle, British Columbia	United States Canada	1962	Temporary agreement for flooding. Interim payment of $5,000/yr
City of Seattle (Utility), British Columbia	United States Canada	1967 opposition since 1970	Formal compensation agreement ($34,566/yr or $7/acre) for leasing of areas flooded in Canada by a lake reservoir in the United States (High Ross–Skagit)
Connecticut, Massachusetts, Maine, New Hampshire, New York, Rhode Island, Vermont Quebec, New Brunswick	United States Canada	1949	Agreement concerning fire fighting through the North-Eastern Forest Fire Protection Commission (U.S. congressional consent, 1949; Canadian approval, 1970)
Maine, Quebec	United States Canada	1975	Forests, etc.
Minnesota, Manitoba	United States Canada	6/3/65 25/9/69	Co-operative agreement on forest fire fighting
Minnesota, Ontario	United States Canada	1/1/73	Memorandum of understanding on forest fire fighting
Montana, Alberta	United States Canada		Arrangement on co-ordinate the combat of forest fire
Washington, British Columbia	United States Canada	22/4/52 19/8/60	Letter of co-operation on border forest fire fighting
Vermont, Ontario, Quebec, New Brunswick, Nova Scotia, Prince Edward Island, Newfoundland	United States Canada	June 1939 March 1972	Cooperation and exchange of ideas in "Forest Insect and Disease Management" through the North-Eastern Forest Pest Council

Source: OECD, *Environmental Protection in Frontier Regions* (Paris: Organization for Economic Cooperation and Development, 1979), pp. 88–90. Reprinted with permission.

understanding was signed by the senior author and the deputy prime minister of Quebec, Gerard Levesque, committing joint funding for the development of exchange programs in the areas of economics, education, cultural affairs, youth, and communications. Maine and Quebec discovered they had a strong interest in cultural and educational exchanges, an interest that could be used as a step toward preservation of the French-speaking culture. In addition, an important dialogue was begun in the field of energy, including oil and electric power, deep water ports, refineries, pipelines, interregional electrical networks, and the bulk sale of electricity.

Much of the interaction between Maine and Nova Scotia has transpired on a regional basis involving all the Maritime provinces; however, discussions were held in Halifax involving direct Maine–Nova Scotia interests such as fisheries and tourism. Two ferries now operate between Yarmouth, Nova Scotia, and Portland, Maine, and the Nova Scotia government operates a large tourist information office in Portland to answer inquiries from all parts of the United States. Both of these accomplishments are at least partly a result of the earlier state-provincial initiatives.

Not to be overlooked, and perhaps most important, are the many benefits that accrue from the establishment of a candid, friendly dialogue between state and provincial leaders. Two practical case examples come readily to mind.

In the first instance, the promoter of a northeast oil refinery suggested to the senior author that he was leaning toward the establishment of a facility in New Brunswick, and he suggested to Premier Hatfield that a site was under consideration in Maine. Instead of engaging in strong competition, the governor of Maine and the premier of New Brunswick discussed the soundness of the proposed project and discovered that both had reservations. As a result, neither Maine nor New Brunswick made any effort to attract the facility. The refinery was later built in another Canadian province, ran into financial difficulty, and is currently inoperative. Close state-provincial communications thus avoided unnecessary competition and its resulting bad feelings as well as the attendant costs and suffering of a business failure.

Another instance of cooperation occurred as a result of the 1973 OPEC oil embargo. A Great Northern Paper Company mill in Millinocket, Maine, employing several hundred people, obtained its industrial oil from the Irving Oil Company refinery in Saint John, New Brunswick. A Canadian federal order to halt further exports, as a means of protecting Canadian supplies, would have quickly resulted in the shutdown of the Maine mill and the layoff of workers with few job alternatives. The direct intervention of Premier Hatfield upon the request of the senior author led to the granting of an export permit and thus the preservation of the Maine jobs.

New England Regional Efforts

The most publicized initiative involving the state of Maine and the Canadian provinces was the formalization of the Conference of New England Governors and Eastern Canadian Premiers in Charlottetown, Prince Edward Island, in 1973. The first action of this conference was the passage of a resolution agreeing to "establish a permanent committee, with representatives from each state and province, as a vehicle to exchange information and to relate the projected energy surpluses of the eastern provinces with the energy needs of the New England States, consistent with the environmental standards of both regions."[8] The Northeast International Committee on Energy was established in 1978 to carry out this mandate. This conference has continued to meet annually and has organized staff activity throughout the year.

The following year, the conference adopted a strong energy resolution aimed at the federal governments, by agreeing to

mutually pledge our individual and collective efforts to persuade our national governments that by international agreement they should create a favorable climate for long-term, secure private and public contracts governing the steady flow of energy, and the full utilization of the most efficient forms of energy production and transportation between the regions represented by the five Eastern Provinces and the New England states.[9]

In the years since, these regional collective efforts toward joint international energy policy for the two regions have intensified, and the annual conference of governors and premiers has strengthened the regional voice. This conference has continued to meet annually and energy has remained the focal point of each agenda. Whether the conference will ultimately make a difference remains to be seen.

On June 27, 1979, the Northeast International Committee on Energy (NICE) was formed. The committee is composed of a representative who is involved in energy-related work from each state and province and was charged "to provide a mechanism for the review, by officials, on energy matters common to the six New England states and five Eastern Canadian Provinces."[10] The junior author represented New Hampshire on the NICE Committee from 1979 to 1981.

This committee has remained active. It sponsors conferences such as those held in 1981 examining the status of conventional fossil fuels and alternative renewable sources of energy. The committee also publishes, as a planning tool, a regional energy data book containing current information on the energy mix and consumption patterns in each state and province.

The early 1980s have witnessed increased interest in bringing Canadian power to New England. Specifically, the governors and premiers have focused on a great deal of activity between the New England Power Pool (the market) and Hydro Quebec (the source of supply) and the related need for new transmission facilities. It seems evident that energy matters alone will continue to dominate the activities of the Eastern Canadian Premiers and New England Governors Conference until at least the end of this century. Given energy's central importance, it alone will probably insure the continued existence of this transnational linkage of subnational governments.

Perhaps one of the more unique arrangements coming out of this conference was the establishment of The International Tourism Regional Foundation, which is a mechanism established "to undertake joint promotion of tourism to the common benefit of New England, Atlantic Canada and Quebec."[11] More specifically, the new agency was designed to "conduct common marketing research, develop marketing policies, and stimulate, encourage and progressively involve interested agencies or organizations in the marketing of tourism in the region at the international level."[12] As a result, there is today a high level of synchronization in tourism policy and reduced competition within the region.

Regional Examples Across the Continent

The Conference of Great Lakes Premiers and Midwest Governors contributed to the successful completion of the 1972 Great Lakes Water Quality Agreement, which was renewed in 1978, and deserves credit for achieving the climate of cooperation necessary to clean up the Great Lakes. Municipal, provincial, and particularly Montana State government officials provided the major stimulus for the creation of a bilateral commission to monitor the environmental effects of the construction and operation of a large fossil-fuel-generating facility located on the Poplar River, in Saskatchewan, just north of the Montana–Saskatchewan border.

What New England governors and Eastern Canadian premiers have established with their transborder efforts serves as a model that is being used or attempted in other regions. The governors of Washington and Alaska, the premier of British Columbia, and the commissioner of the Yukon territorial government have been meeting periodically for a number of years to discuss issues and concerns common to the region, from transportation and energy, to economic development and environmental questions, to fisheries and other mutual concerns. Furthermore, Alberta and Montana have been trying to interest Saskatchewan and neighboring Rocky Mountain and Plains states to follow the New England–Eastern Canadian model. Western governors have, in fact, recently invited Western Canadian Premiers to join their meetings. Ontario and Michigan, likewise, occasionally express a desire to form a permanent Great Lakes group along similar lines; and the governor of Michigan and premier of Ontario have recently held meetings to accomplish this objective. There have also been meetings of the Ontario premier and governors of the Great Lakes states.

The states and provinces interact in other formal ways. Several states have opened state development offices in Canada, and there are several provincial investment and trade offices in American cities. The Quebec government is particularly active in establishing government offices in various U.S. cities, and Ontario and Alberta are showing increasing tendencies to follow suit.

Although the most extensive relationships exist within the executive branches, cross-border interaction also occurs between the states and provinces at the legislative level. The state of Maine has an active Maine-Canadian Legislative Advisory Office that reports directly to the legislative branch. Quebec has engaged in several legislative exchanges with states that have large French-speaking populations. The Washington state legislature has held joint meetings with their British Columbia counterparts; and the state and province have made several attempts to formalize a legislative relationship. Both the Legislative Assembly in British Columbia and the Washington state legislature have expressed intentions of forming a permanent, informal liaison committee between the two bodies. Following a joint legislative conference held in September, 1973, the Washington state Senate adopted a resolution establishing a joint Senate-House committee called The Joint Legislative Committee on Washington/British Columbia Cooperation. The plan for British Columbia to adopt a similar resolution was never formalized, but, nevertheless, the intent of the resolution carried forward.

It has been the experience of the senior author that the most effective interactions are really those based upon a handshake rather than upon written, unenforceable agreements. Numbers of largely unreported incidents of cooperation occur on a daily basis between municipal officials of both countries. Such efforts are built upon personal relations as a practical means of managing the problems of close co-existence. The formal agreements or, more correctly, memoranda of understanding, establish a climate and sometimes provide structure; but the personal relations and the will that lies behind them will carry the day.

The Federal Presence

All of the above examples raise this question: how can subnational levels of two governments work together and reach agreement in a manner so seemingly outside of the federal jurisdiction? The fact that this occurs at all is based on pragmatic terms and is a tribute to the U.S.-Canadian relationship. The respective federal governments simply could not manage the multitude of day-to-day needs that occur. The U.S. Constitution clearly limits the power to make treaties to the president, with the advice and consent of the U.S. Senate. Article I, section 10, is even more prohibitive to the negotiation of state-provincial agreements in declaring that "[n]o state shall enter into any treaty, alliance or confederation.... No state shall, without the consent of Congress... enter into any agreement or compact with another state or with a foreign power...."[13]

But the interactions discussed in this chapter are not "compacts," although some might be thought of as "agreements." More correctly, they are memoranda of understanding. Arguably, they are not binding, thus removing them from the constitutional restraint. They are founded on good will, as are the cross-border subnational relationships. The eighty-eighth session of Congress, recognizing that the states understand their local problems better than the federal government, clarified the requirement for consent, stating:

> the terms "compact" and "agreement"... do not apply to every compact or agreement... but the prohibition is directed to the formulation of any combination tending to the increase of political power in the states which may encroach upon or interfere with the just supremacy of the United States. The terms cover all stipulations affecting the conduct or claims of states, whether verbal or written, formal or informal, positive or implied, with each other or with foreign powers.[14]

In Canada, there are similar restrictions. However, the Canadian Department of External Affairs has recognized the greater autonomy of the provinces and their need to become involved in areas of international interaction; it only limits them to "arrangements subsumed under agreements between Canada and the foreign government concerned," or "administrative arrangements of an informal character... not subject to international law."[15]

As a result of this federal recognition on both sides of the border, many formal interactions have been permitted to occur between the states and provinces, between the provinces and the U.S. government, between U.S. states and the Canadian federal goverment, and between some municipalities. Many such interactions logically address border transportation needs, such as toll bridges and ferries and other practical necessities.

In 1980, the U.S. State Department recognized the importance of state and provincial interactions by assigning, on an experimental basis, a senior foreign service officer to serve as a liaison between the U.S. Embassy in Ottawa and the Provincial Co-ordination Division of the Department of External Affairs. The Reagan administration subsequently abolished this office and substituted an Office of Intergovernmental Affairs to provide a liaison between the State Department and U.S. local and state governments. There are also Canadian foreign service officers at the embassy in Washington doing largely provincial interest work.

Conclusion

In a day-to-day relationship as extensive as that of the United States and Canada, informal interactions at the subnational level are essential, and their effectiveness has been demonstrated. The Honorable Richard Hatfield, a veteran premier of New Brunswick, provided the best summation in a statement prepared for the Canadian Senate Standing Committee on Foreign Affairs on February 20, 1975:

> ...the impetus to do more must come from the states and provinces themselves, by identifying areas of common interest and concern, by assisting one another when possible and by cooperating with one another when cooperation will yield mutual benefit. Some things we can do among ourselves as states and provinces. Others are beyond the joint competence of provincial and state governments because of the wide economic, financial and constitutional powers of the respective federal governments. On these matters, it is my view, at least, that agreements or determinations entered into jointly by the states and provinces should be brought jointly by these states and provinces to the attention of both national administrations. In this way, the necessary inter-relationships on which the determinations are based will be placed in context and both federal governments will have an opportunity to assess their implications and take action, if appropriate, in a manner which will be to the greatest advantage of the larger province-state region.[16]

The evolution of Canadian federal-provincial relations and the success of U.S. administrations to transfer more power to the states will undoubtedly have a bearing on the future success or failure of these regional provincial-state cross-border initiatives. For the time being, at least, the two coastal groupings, Atlantic and Pacific, are likely to continue their efforts, their achievements largely determined by the rise and fall of individual key governors and premiers and the level of interest that both maintain.

Notes

1. See Kenneth M. Curtis, "Shaping the Canadian–United States Dialogue—A Truly Democratic Process," paper presented to Harvard University's Canadian Studies Seminar, April 27, 1982.

2. "Canada–United States Relations," vol. 1, "The Institutional Framework for the Relationship," Standing Senate Committee on Foreign Affairs, December 1975, p. 29.

3. Roger Swanson, *State/Provincial Interaction—A Study of Relations Between U.S. States and Canadian Provinces Prepared for the U.S. Department of State* (Washington.: Office of External Research, Bureau of Intelligence and Research, Department of State, (Contract 1722-320061, August, 1974).

4. Joint agreement between state of Maine and province of New Brunswick, June 28, 1973, p. 1, preamble.

5. *Ibid.*

6. *Ibid.*, p. 1, resolve.

7. Ibid.

8. Energy Resolution of the New England Governors and Eastern Canadian Premiers, Conference of Eastern Canadian Premiers and New England Governors, Prince Edward Island, August 16-17, 1973, para. 5.

9. Sugarbush Compact between the Governors of the New England States and the Premiers of Eastern Canada, June 14, 1974, resolve.

10. Joint Resolution of the New England Governors and Eastern Canadian Premiers regarding the program of the Northeast International Committee on Energy, Ville d'Esterel, Quebec, June 27, 1979.

11. International Tourism Region, Eighth Annual Conference, New England Governors and Eastern Canadian Premiers, June 27, 1980.

12. *Ibid.*

13. U.S. Constitution, art. I, sec. 10.

14. U.S. Senate Document 39, 88th Congress, 1st sess.

15. Canada, Department of External Affairs, "Federalism and International Relations" (Ottawa: Queens Printer, 1968), as quoted in R.F. Swanson, *Inter-governmental Perspectives on the Canada-U.S. Relationship* (New York: New York University Press, 1975).

16. Senate of Canada, Proceedings of the Standing Committee on Foreign Affairs, Issue no. 7, Thursday, February 20, 1975, p. 7:6, Evidence given by Hon. Richard Hatfield, Premier of New Brunswick.

8 The Private Relationship

All parts of the United States and Canada can be reached by direct-dialing from either country, just as if the call were being placed within one nation. Residents of the United States can telephone residents of Canada, and be called by them, as easily as they can telephone friends and neighbors. For most of history, mail crossing the border has been treated by both countries as domestic mail and subject only to domestic postal rates. Except for customs, driving or flying across the border is no more difficult than moving from state to state or province to province. Many fine roads in both nations lead to and cross the border, and interstate and interprovincial highways are directly connected. Transborder commercial flights are numerous. Most Canadian cities are within 150 miles of the border, which facilitates the exposure of the Canadian people to American ways. Except for the linguistic differences along the northern New England–Quebec border region, the people do not differ in any noticeable way from each other. This similarity is reinforced by an extensive exchange of television and radio programs carried by the numerous transmitters serving near-border populations. Finally, a lack of trade barriers translates into a minimal interruption or disincentive to the free flow of most goods from one nation to the other.

Is it surprising, therefore, that an extensive nongovernmental, nonpublic, and therefore private relationship between the people of these two nations has flourished? If for no other reason than its vastness and complexity, this private relationship can be viewed as not only nongovernmental but as outside the sphere and control of government. Furthermore, the character of this private relationship can influence the public and even the formal diplomatic relationship, as has been demonstrated with environmental issues.

To some extent, the reality of transborder relations, their quantity and constancy, reduces the traditional role of diplomats. They deal with extensive intergovernmental relationships, but private contact is well beyond their means even to monitor, much less manage or control. In recent decades practice has reinforced not only the freedom of the private entrepreneur and citizen, but also the ease with which public officials not connected to the Department of State or the Department of External Affairs communicate with their counterparts across the border, almost as if they were their own colleagues. (The tendency of Canadian scientists and officials to take their graduate degrees in American universities once supported an old boy network that ignored the boundary, but this era is passing with the significant expansion of graduate education in Canada.)

The U.S. and Canadian societies are full of examples of cross-border affiliations of one type or another that represent efforts either to capture the markets of one side or the other (for example, Ford Motor Company and Ford, Canada, Ltd.) or to win membership in a joint cause (as by various civic, fraternal, and religious organizations and labor unions). Multitudes of such entities are now functioning, all ignoring the existence of the border to a greater or lesser degree. Some are national entities, others regional or local entities. Most are dominated by Americans (and generally initiated by them), although the Canadian presence, particularly in business and investment, is being felt increasingly south of the border.

An especially interesting phenomenon has been the development of active private groups designed to join in common cause to resolve bilateral problems or alleviate their effects. Examples include groups as diverse as the Canadian-American Committee of the (U.S.) National Planning Association and the (Canadian) C.D. Howe Institute, as well as the U.S.-Canadian committees of the two national chambers of commerce (in the business field), and the Canada-U.S. Environment Committee (CUSEC) in the environmental, wilderness, and wildlife field.

Private Joint Endeavors: Three Examples

At least three examples of private joint endeavors deserve mention. One in environmentalism (CUSEC), one in academia (the Association for Canadian Studies in the United States, or ACSUS), and one in business (the Canadian-American Committee, or CAC) illustrate the scope of the institutionalized bilateral relationship in three very different areas.

Canada-U.S. Environment Committee

In the early 1970s, during the height of what has been called the era of environmentalism in North America, several U.S. and Canadian environmental organizations became aware of an array of international wilderness and wildlife issues, Arctic and marine issues, and transboundary environmental problems about which they shared similar views and concerns. Based in the Wilderness Society in Washington and the Canadian Nature Federation in Ottawa, the Canada-U.S. Environment Committee counts in its membership as many as twenty or thirty national and regional organizations, including the Sierra Club, Friends of the Earth, the National Audubon Society, Friends of the Boundary Waters Wilderness, and other well-known American national and regional groups; and Canada's Pollution Probe, Energy Probe, Friends of the Earth–Canada, the Alberta Wilderness Association, and others. All are joined under the CUSEC umbrella in common cause to protect environmental interests. The central thrust of these groups is the protection of wilderness, wilderness-type wildlife such as caribou, wilderness parks, endangered species, and Arctic and marine ecosystems—in other words, the wild places of the continent that happen to be near the international border on land or sea. Interest in environmental problems closer to home, such as water pollution and air pollution, is present but of lesser priority. Budgeted on a shoestring, CUSEC has managed to convene at least one meeting each year, alternating between the two countries. The product of these meetings, aside from the widely publicized resolutions taken on various issues, is the opportunity for American and Canadian environmentalist leaders to get acquainted, to better understand each other's country, and, perhaps most important, to plan a common transborder strategy. Although the greatest impact has been felt in the wilderness–wildlife–parks area, CUSEC's recent attention to acid rain and the revision of the U.S. Clean Air Act may denote a move into the wider arena of environmental quality. Broader transborder alliances may well result, further weakening the reality of the border's existence.

Association for Canadian Studies in the United States

Another product of the early 1970s is academia's Association for Canadian Studies in the United States. Formed with strong support from the U.S. Donner Foundation, the Canadian government, and, in the early 1980s, the Exxon Foundation, ACSUS derives the majority of its membership from faculty members of small American colleges and universities, both public and private. Strongest regionally in the Northeast (for example, at the universities of Vermont and Maine, State University of New York and St. Lawrence University), this organization's membership and the institutions represented is expanding throughout the United States and even into regions far removed from Canada. Its academic base lies in private liberal arts colleges and in the liberal arts departments of state universities, with political science, history, geography, and literature being among the best represented disciplines. ACSUS has so far garnered few members or support from applied disciplines such as business, agriculture, natural resources, engineering, or public affairs, nor has it achieved significant success in the very large universities. Nevertheless, it enjoys firm support from the Canadian government, its embassy, and its many consulates general in the United States. The organization publishes an academic journal *(The American Review of Canadian Studies)* and a newsletter; it also holds a biennial meeting that attracts sizeable numbers of scholars. Organizationally, it is becoming a strong link between the two countries, while performing its primary mission of educating those who educate future generations of Americans on all matters Canadian.

Canadian-American Committee

The Canadian-American Committee was established in 1957 to study the broad range of economic factors affecting the bilateral relationship. Its membership, at the level of chief executive officer or senior vice president, is drawn largely from the corporate business sector of both nations, but also includes representation from labor and agriculture. Without exception, its members have direct involvement, experience, and interest in the bilateral relationship.

The committee is sponsored in the United States by the National Planning Association in Washington and in Canada by the C.D. Howe Research Institute in Toronto. It meets semi-annually, alternating between the two countries and convening in geographically diverse cities so that it might focus on regional as well as national bilateral concerns. Views are exchanged, members' individual positions are formulated, and ways are sought to resolve bilateral problems. The committee sponsors research on bilateral matters and provides a forum and sounding board for its membership. It helps create the proper atmosphere for the development of numerous transborder relationships and linkages. While its major interests are in trade, investment, finance, and the general economic relationship, it has in recent years expanded its scope to other issues that affect bilateral relations, including water resources, fisheries, and acid rain. The significance of this committee as an important factor in transborder business relations capable of fostering the health of that relationship should not be underestimated. While the committee does not lobby as such, it can play a crucial role in influencing those who do.

The Impact of Private Actors: An Environmental Example

Traditionally, negotiation and settlement of international differences, including those related to the environment, are primarily the domain of government officials in the countries concerned. The last decade, however, has witnessed a rapidly increasing role for organized private citizens in local, regional, national, and international nongovernmental groups. Somewhat to the consternation of their governments, these groups often do not recognize international boundaries; their orientation is centered more in the ecological health of the environment than in the economic or political concerns of their own country. Such environmental groups have been proliferating in number, manpower, and resources. The sophistication with which many of these groups, particularly those south of the border, oppose projects on environmental grounds and influence political and bureaucratic decision makers at relevant levels of government, both directly and through pertinent segments of public opinion, has increased considerably since the 1960s. The changed climate of public opinion regarding environmental priorities, especially in the United States, has been largely due to the efforts of these nongovernmental groups.

Though specific tactics of these groups have varied with the issue in question, most transborder issues evoke all or most of the following:

General airing of the issue, stressing its environmental aspects, to as wide an audience as possible, through public demonstrations and other activities apt to attract mass media coverage, and through articles, announcements, brief newsletters, and other printed materials in their own magazines and in mailings to key people in media, voluntary organizations, and governments.

On-site demonstrations and other actions designed to prevent or frustrate construction and/or operation of the project and to project their arguments to a wider public.

Intervening legally via court injunctions and lawsuits (mainly in the United States).

Identifying and then enlisting the cooperation of potential allies in both countries to broaden and intensify impacts on influential segments of opinion and government reached by their arguments.

Getting the broadest possible support of persuasive petitions and other communication directed at decision makers.

Pinpointing key governmental actors—congressmen, senators, members of parliament and provincial legislative assemblies, agency bureaucrats, and embassy officials—and organizing coordinated letter, telegram, telephone, and face-to-face campaigns to maximize pressure on them, including bringing such pressure to bear in the electoral districts of key legislators.

Working with comparable key private groups in the other country in collaborative action and facilitating the exchange of pertinent information about both substance and tactics across the frontier. Such collaboration has provided both private and governmental actors at local, provincial-state, and national levels with materials developed in the other country, such as reports on hearings, testimonies, and petitions; joint analyses of the opposition's weaknesses; joint strategy planning sessions; and frequent transborder telephone consultation. Approaches to key local, state, and federal officials have increasingly been synchronized by U.S. groups with Canadian approaches to their governmental counterparts.

In the mid and late 1970s U.S. environmentalists were searching for Canadian support in order to oppose Canadian developmental projects that were believed to be threatening to the U.S. environment. The early 1980s have witnessed a reversal of these roles, with Canadian environmentalists seeking support in Washington and in concerned border states in achieving acid rain controls in U.S. legislation. The particular coalition of environmentalist groups and its leadership, both in the United States and across the border, have varied with the issue.

Many local, state, and regional organizations have been involved, particularly on the U.S. side, in these efforts. They have typically been active, however, only for brief periods of time, and on issues having direct local impacts. Some have been hastily organized, one-issue groups, designed to oppose and focus attention on a particular threat. These have usually withered or disappeared when the threat appeared to terminate. Their central thrust is to quickly alert people of the area to possible negative environmental impacts, to influence local congressmen and other elected officials, and to press appropriate federal bureaucrats. Occasionally their aim has been litigation, if they have the financial means and talent, or cooperation with one or more other local and/or national groups in litigation.

Effective court litigation has been much more feasible under the U.S. than the Canadian judicial system. One major reason for the greater influence of U.S. environmentalists is the fact that they do have standing to sue, to bring class action litigation, a right that Canadians do not have. U.S. groups are thus much more likely to use legal vehicles while their Canadian allies utilize informational, propaganda, and "educational" means and related political actions. In general, the Canadian citizens' environmentalist movement is small, weak, and poorly organized in comparison with its U.S. counterpart. It also lacks the sophistication that has increasingly characterized the behavior of at least the larger, more professional, more enduring, and more effective U.S. groups.

Thus parallel action and cooperation across the border, insofar as it has taken place, was until recently initiated by U.S. groups and characterized by short-term arrangements tailored to the individual issue, with differing organizational composition from issue to issue. In the decade of the 1980s, attention shifted from the border to Washington; and transnational environmental coalitions are now a reality influencing, at least to some degree, the conduct of the U.S.-Canadian relationship.

Some Thoughts on the Cultural Relationship:
A Francophone Example

The private relationship of the United States and Canada is far more complex than the interaction of those nongovernmental bilateral groups, however important they may be. The crux of the private relationship is felt in tangible and intangible daily interaction that constantly adds richness to the culture of this continent. The maintenance of the French-speaking culture in North America is one aspect of the intangible values involved and is, additionally, an example of Canadian cultural influence in the United States. A large population of French-speaking descent reside in the United States, historically concentrated throughout the New England states and in Louisiana. Recently, numerous exchange programs initiated primarily by the province of Quebec have stimulated a commitment in those states to preserve their French-speaking heritage, a richness that could otherwise be lost in a country that rapidly absorbs diverse cultures.

Francophones in New England in recent years have become more cognizant of their French-Canadian tradition. Consequently, there has been an observable effort to re-learn or re-capture the traditions of the culture and even the language. These are exemplified in such organizations as the Institute of French and Franco-American Studies at Assumption College in Worcester, Massachusetts, the Franco-American Resources Opportunity Group (also known as the FAROG Forum) at the University of Maine, and the New Hampshire Franco-American Council in Manchester, New Hampshire; in the publication and distribution of French language books and other materials; in the convening of conferences; and in television programming.

French influence on this continent dates back to 1604, when Samuel de Champlain organized the first colony at the mouth of the St. Croix River on what is today the Maine-New Brunswick border. From that time on, France moved quickly to extend its presence from Montreal west to the Mississippi and south to New Orleans; and the ensuing military conflicts, treaties, and purchases that led to the establishment of an international boundary never erased that early and continuing French influence.

Hard economic times in Quebec and the industrial revolution brought Quebecers to the mill towns of New England. Between 1840 and 1930 more than a million Quebecers moved to the United States. While we tend to associate our French-speaking heritage with that province, a sizeable number of Franco-Americans come from Acadian ancestry, with roots in what are now the Canadian Maritime provinces (New Brunswick, Nova Scotia, Prince Edward Island) and in a portion of northern Maine.

Large numbers of Franco-Americans, nearly 20 percent of the population, still live in Maine. In 1973, this heritage prompted the senior author, who was then governor of Maine, and Quebec's vice prime minister, Gerard D. Levesque, to sign an official statement[1] agreeing to and jointly funding several exchange programs as a first step toward a formalized effort to preserve the French-speaking culture in Maine. In the field of education, it was agreed to grant an initial thirty scholarships to Maine students for an intensive French language study program at the Centre Linguistique de

Saguenay, and to institute an exchange of professors of second language from the state and province.

Culturally, a large Quebec festival was held in Maine featuring films, theatre, and folklore; a research project was planned involving three Canadian and U.S. universities to collect material on the cultural traditions of Acadian origin in the Madawaska region of Maine and New Brunswick; and Maine professors of French were assigned to a course on Quebec studies. In addition, groundwork was laid for an eventual exchange of research graduate students between the University of Maine and the Université du Quebec; and the Maine Public Broadcasting Network initiated discussions with Radio Quebec in the areas of programming and technical development.

The Quebec provincial government continues to stimulate such cultural activity throughout New England and other regions. For example, a reading of a press synopsis of activities for just one week reported the standing ovation received by the Montreal Symphony Orchestra while performing at Carnegie Hall; announced the opening of an exhibition of the works of 21 Quebec artists at the Boston Public Library; announced the award of summer fellowships to U.S. universities for doctoral research on Canada; and reported a New England–Quebec student exchange program involving twenty-two New England institutions and ten Quebec universities. It is clear, therefore, that there is a determination among the New England Francophone community, rooted in a feeling of pride, to preserve their cultural heritage.[2]

Some Concluding Thoughts

The private U.S.-Canadian relationship, operating at all levels of both societies, yields tangible benefits impacting upon the well-being of people on both sides of the border. It is conceivable that no two nations have experienced the level of cultural and economic integration achieved by the Canadian and American peoples along a long and diversified border. This involvement is based in the blood kinship shared by the two peoples; the fact that large numbers of the nationals of each nation live in the other nation; the high level of economic integration and interdependency; the common ethnic heritage; and the common religious and social values. The ready and constant cross-border association in conferences and meetings of engineers, scientists and other professionals from both nations, and the positive contribution to society that results from that contact, also foster transnational community.

Recent times have seen a literal invasion of Canada by American mass media and, concomitantly, American pop culture. Many Canadians view more American television than their own, read more American publications than their own, and are influenced by American motion pictures, music, and humor. The inundation of Canadian society by U.S. taste and lifestyle represented in electronic media has been vigorously rejected by some Canadians while it is embraced and demanded by others even in preference to their own. Until recently, Canadians chose American universities for their advanced postgraduate and professional training far more than their own. Sometimes, of course, these choices are made because of the greater variety available in the U.S. market rather than because of a desire to avoid opportunities at home. Attraction to variety is natural, but it has led to loss of Canadian identity and of things distinctively "Canadian."

This dilemma of choice has yet to sort itself out; but the loud call of nationalists and other groups concerned about the protection of Canadian cultural identity has been heard. With the passage of legislation requiring "Canadian content" as well as the passage of laws discriminating against U.S. and other "foreign content" in one form or another, Canada embarked in the 1960s and 1970s on a course clearly different from that previously pursued.

Canadians are aware of the positive and negative balance of the U.S. influence. Few Americans are aware, however, of the Canadian influence on their daily lives, an influence out of proportion to that nation's small population. Canada, for example, has exported to the United States such things as standard time, ice hockey, the snowmobile, the zipper, kerosene, the telephone, and new scientific technology. The list of U.S.-Canadian transborder linkages and influences of a nongovernmental nature is endless. In all, they make the bilateral relationship between these two nations a most unusual international relationship, and in all likelihood define that relationship to a greater extent than do those charged with formal government-to-government diplomatic relations, a unique situation in international diplomacy.

The vast, atypical nature of this private, nongovernmental relationship ensures that U.S.-Canadian relations are not effectively controlled by government or by diplomats but rather have a dynamic of their own. To the extent the relationship is managed, that management is widely shared by diplomats; by a diverse collection of federal, state, and provincial politicians; by an equally diverse array of business and financial interests; by varied citizen organizations, by the media; and by that tremendous number of private citizens who drive or fly across the border or, even more simply, pick up the telephone and dial.

Thus the nongovernmental relationship defies easy analysis or categorization. Certain subtle (and not so subtle) factors are also important: the perception each people has about the other; and the fact that the ignorance of the American people concerning Canadians is greater than Canadian ignorance about the United States. Indeed, as many studies have shown, most Americans do not even know the fundamentals of Canadian geography, the names of the nation's leaders, or the moving forces of the society. It has been said that American knowledge and understanding of Canada is necessary to good U.S.-Canadian relations. The Canadian Senate's Standing

Committee on Foreign Affairs concluded its 1975 report on "Canada-United States Relations: The Institutional Framework for the Relationship" with this thought: "Good Canadian-American relations depend ultimately on American knowledge and understanding of Canada."

Some isolationists may argue that Americans do not need to have this knowledge; that strategically Canada's destiny is linked to that of the United States; and that, therefore, knowledge of the nation north of the border by the nation south of the border is not necessary. Whether this is a safe assumption now or will be in the future are questions Americans must ponder. The authors side with those who believe continued ignorance will be costly, to this generation and to future ones.

Notes

1. Official statement following the meeting of Maine and Quebec officials, Augusta, Maine, June 10-11, 1973.

2. For an up-to-date analysis of Quebec-U.S. cultural linkages, among others, see Alfred O. Hero and Marcel Daneau, eds., *Problems and Opportunities in U.S.-Quebec Relations* (Boulder, Colorado: Westview Press, 1983).

9   Summary

Chapter 2 outlined the politics and diplomacy of U.S.-Canadian relations, focusing on the history of the relationship, its evolution to the present, the process and structure of U.S.-Canadian diplomacy, and some of the principal points of agreement and disagreement characterizing the contemporary relationship. It closed with the differing world-views of the two nations, as well as military and strategic considerations.

For the past decade the prime minister of Canada has had a deep interest and forceful opinions relative to the North-South debate in global politics. His record indicates a strong empathy with the need of the peoples of Africa, Asia, and Latin America to break the shackles of their poverty. His and his country's identification with the French-speaking peoples of the world further enhances that empathy; and the promotion of Canada as a major actor in working bilaterally, and also multilaterally through international organizations, to improve the prospects of the many Third World LDCs (less developed countries) has been a major goal of his government—and one that appears to have substantial political support throughout Canada.

Rarely has a U.S. administration had such a deep general identification with the Third World as has Canada. The Reagan administration places its priorities on East-West rather than North-South concerns, leading to greater interest in the activities of the Soviet Union and its allies than in the concerns of other nations. This emphasis has placed the United States in a very different niche from that of Canada in the eyes of many of the world's peoples. One defense of this policy, which is partially justified, is that this difference is natural, given the role of the United States as protector and defender of both the continent and the free world.[1] Canada, unburdened by this responsibility and automatically defended by the United States, has the luxury to pursue a more independent path.

Whatever the merits of this argument, the divergent roles of the two nations inevitably lead to diplomatic problems. Canada and the United States are finding themselves more and more often at odds with one another over foreign policy. Canada's early recognition of China (1970), its uninterrupted recognition of Cuba, its antipathy toward U.S. policy in Vietnam, and, more recently, its clear lack of sympathy for the U.S. stance on El Salvador are some of the signals of deeper differences between these two peoples and their views of the world. A trend may be developing toward greater Canadian global integration concurrent with increasing U.S. isolationism, as suggested in chapter 2, from even its traditional allies. Historically, such a pattern has occurred before, but not without negative consequences.

Chapter 3 highlighted the fact that Canada and the United States are each other's best trading partners. It described the bilateral economic relationship as a complex one of dependence and interdependence that is extremely important for the future of each nation. It addressed approaches toward free trade, the Auto Pact, trade protectionism, U.S. reliance on Canadian raw materials, Canadian reliance on U.S. markets, and Canada's desire for what it calls its third option, coupled with its consequent efforts to diversify trading partners.

There will always be in U.S.-Canadian trade relations a substantial amount of competition, most of it healthy for both economies. There will also be many opportunities for mutual trade endeavors that will bring greater net benefits to both peoples than either could achieve alone. The current trend toward virtual free trade by the next decade is desirable as long as Canada's economic identity can be maintained. Americans must learn to respect Canada's legitimate (and quite natural) desire to "Canadianize" (that is, enhance Canadian ownership and control) of vital sectors of its economy, such as energy. Americans must also understand Canada's legitimate desire to reduce its economic dependence on the United States by substituting for this dependence new trade linkages with other industrialized and industrializing areas of the world. Such diversification is not only in the interests of a healthier Canada (and thereby a healthier North America) but may also ultimately open new windows for U.S. entrepreneurs, based on the positive position Canada is developing in the eyes of those nations. Thus, in the long term, the United States may benefit from a resurrection of what Canada once called its third option toward trade independence.

Chapter 4 treated those common continental concerns that result from a common geography and force a sharing of resources. Attention was devoted to such issues as environmental quality (both air and water), water resource allocation, marine fisheries, marine and coastal pollution, and the unfinished business of four disputed maritime boundaries along with the resource ramifications of these disputes. It also presented differing perspectives on Arctic sovereignty and the environmental and strategic considerations inherent in that debate. Specific case examples of these problems, including the Garrison water diversion and Poplar power plant questions, the Great Lakes challenges, and the serious acid rain dispute, were addressed.

Transboundary environmental problems between the United States and Canada have risen from a historically rather inconsequential position on the bilateral agenda to an important and even at times dominating position. Recognition of this fact has not kept pace with reality, especially in the United States. These matters are no longer narrow technical subjects affecting small numbers in remote border locations. They now represent hundreds, even thousands, of jobs, many millions of dollars, the future of vast un-developed regions, the success or failure of national energy policies, and the future of international export markets. They also represent the willingness to honor sacred treaty obligations, the willingness to show good faith, the basic respect the two peoples have for one another, and, in some instances, the health and welfare of each other's citizens. The current status of U.S.-Canadian environmental relations is an index to the level of honesty and caring each nation shows the other. Both peoples need to become aware of what they are doing to each other environmentally before these issues cause irreversible damage. An increased recognition—through action, not rhetoric—of their differences must come soon, followed by tangible action through a reasonable commitment of resources. Americans and Canadians have lived long enough off the past glory of the Boundary Waters Treaty, the International Joint Commission, the Great Lakes Agreements, and other such accomplishments.

Chapter 5 described the nature of the increasingly complex bilateral energy relationship. The advantages accrued by and the problems pre-sented by past energy exchange, the conflict between Canadian nationalism and future Canadian energy export, and opportunities to be realized from future collaboration were all outlined. Special emphasis was placed on Cana-dian hydroelectricity and natural gas and their future role in bilateral energy relations.

In the late 1970s U.S.-Canadian relations came to be dominated by energy matters and the prospect for joint development of large-scale energy projects. Bright new opportunities began to emerge, particularly in Cana-dian hydroelectricity export; and many new dreams were born, especially in natural gas, outer continental shelf oil, and Alberta tar sands. With the advent of serious economic problems in the 1980s, many of the megascale and frontier projects appeared threatened. Some Canadians began to view the U.S. need as an insatiable thirst for Canadian energy that might ulti-mately deprive future generations of Canadians of this energy (with attend-ant environmental and energy costs). Simultaneously, some Americans began to cynically regard Canada's export plans as an undermining of future U.S. domestic energy production, particularly from coal and nuclear sources. Regardless, it now appears that at least some of the hydroelectricity plans (Hydro Quebec's export to New York and New England) and at least one nuclear export to the U.S. (from New Brunswick to New England) will succeed, while many other large-scale hydrocarbon projects are now in doubt.

Both Americans and Canadians need to realize that energy exchange is a two-way street. Americans need not fear over-reliance on this foreign source because Canadians have just as great a need for U.S. capital to develop the projects, for external markets for the energy, and for cash to strengthen their dollar and sagging economy. Likewise, Canadians need not fear too strongly a U.S. depletion of Canadian energy reserves, because advances in energy technology may well alter the long-term value of these reserves. (Of course, Canadians do need to guard against unnecessary environmental damage and reduce that which must inevitably occur.)

In the total energy picture it is easy to become caught up in the romance and excitement of the megaprojects and the great media attention to them, while forgetting the small, perhaps less dramatic, but regionally crucial bilateral energy opportunities—from potential Canadian storage of U.S. surplus oil product and strategic reserves, to rationalizing the use of oil refineries so as to take advantage of surplus capacity wherever it exists, to many opportunities for the development of new electrical grids enabling small power exchanges when needed. Most important, the two peoples should not ignore the benefits of joint research in the vast and highly significant area of new energy technology, including joint research on ways to reduce the health and environmental costs of energy production.

Chapter 6 described the role of an important and unique institution in the U.S.-Canadian relationship, the International Joint Commission (IJC), its structure, and process. This commission is often cited as a model of how best to conduct bilateral environmental relations. It can be that model. However, as the chapter emphasized, what the commission is and what it could be are two different things. The two federal governments must work to divorce it from national interests, sever the too close links with State and External Affairs, fund it adequately, and give it strong leadership. The record of accomplishment in recent decades has not been what it might have been. It is not good today. Until this fact is more widely recognized by the Canadian and American people, little will likely change. The commission must become better known, its capabilities and potentials must be better realized. There are certainly many notable achievements in the IJC's long history, but to portray it today as a fine model of how to conduct a transboundary environmental relationship is, at the least, misleading. The commission could be so much more than it is. The fact that it isn't is a loss to all of us in both countries.

Chapter 7 focused on the relationships between subnational levels of government, specifically states and provinces. It described the numerous joint programs and arrangements that characterize state-provincial relations and the different relationship each of these entities maintains with its respective federal government. The extensive regional north-south orientation was also noted.

The states and provinces can point the way to improved relations. They can also create serious problems. In the United States the constitutional role of state governments in foreign relations is clear: they do not have a formal role. However, in practice the states do have an informal role to play with their neighbors across the international frontier; they can also undertake a very important role in influencing Washington on the bilateral relationship. These opportunities will undoubtedly be enhanced in coming years, given the current U.S. thrust toward states' rights and home rule.

The position of the provinces is very different. For the most part, they have great expertise in dealing with both the U.S. federal government and the states, often through intergovernmental affairs bureaucracies that are set up for this purpose. Their jurisdiction and authority in international affairs, however, is not as clear as those of their state government counterparts; the authority they claim and the authority Ottawa claims for them are two different things.[2] This discrepancy leads to uneasiness across the border, in both Washington and the states. In terms of corresponding authority, the provinces are often matched, in fact, by Washington rather than by the states. This problem will not be resolved until Canadians settle their domestic problem of federal-provincial relations. Nevertheless, the value of the experience gained through positive state-provincial relations should not be overlooked by the federal governments. Those governments can gain from state-provincial experience so as to enable them to resolve diverse bilateral problems.

Chapter 8 recognized the peculiarly important and extensive role of the private or nongovernmental relationship in day-to-day U.S.-Canadian relations. These nongovernmental entities range from businesses to labor unions, to citizen environmentalist and civic organizations, to academic groups. They play an important and an increasing role and could well become a positive force toward the education of both peoples, as well as bring about the introduction of new principles and practices. Since their interests are almost always transborder and, in fact, do not often recognize the existence of political borders, these groups can be a force for unity, provided the interests they represent are not too narrow.

Any book that depicts the U.S.-Canadian relationship as a typical government-to-government diplomatic relationship, while ignoring the vast, even incomprehensible, and unmanageable relationships that are conducted by these two peoples every hour of the day and night, would be misleading. The diplomatic relationship is dwarfed in comparison to this extensive and on-going private relationship. The lesson to be learned from this reality, however, is at least three-fold: the U.S.-Canadian relationship is unique and therefore not a source for too many precedents to be applied elsewhere; second, size dictates that, although uncoordinated in nature, nongovernmental rather than formal interaction defines the relationship; and, third, government has much to learn from the private sector and would benefit from more formal involvement of that sector in diplomacy.

This chapter brings to the fore the central theme of this book: that the problems that divide us are becoming increasingly serious, that there are real opportuniites to achieve mutually beneficial goals of great magnitude, and that these very opportunities can be placed at risk and perhaps be lost with further deterioration in bilateral relations.

Chapter 10 presents the authors' recommendations in the form of a prescription for future action, a program that would seek to avoid further ruptures, maintain good relations, and keep options open for future collaboration. It calls specifically for the development in Washington of a "New Canada Policy", a broad all-encompassing plan to govern the future of U.S.-Canadian relations in the remaining years of this century and beyond.

Notes

1. Others would argue in a very different way. One Canadian official has remarked to the authors, "I think Canada, reflecting its greater domestic concern with the less advantaged, is fundamentally more interested in social progress and stability based on social justice than is the U.S., where the 'guns don't kill people' ethic easily translates into easy involvement in El Salvador."

2. A Canadian official reflects, "Even what Ottawa likes, however, is far more than the states can get; in acid rain talks, the provinces are fully integrated in the Canadian delegation and in the Work Groups. The states aren't even told what's going on."

10 A Prescription for Future Action

The basic prerequisite for maintaining a healthier U.S.-Canadian relationship should be structured from two basic fundamentals: a clear, well-articulated commitment from the president, the prime minister, and their respective governments to its overriding importance; and a greater understanding in both countries of the rich benefits of that relationship.

We believe that good U.S.-Canadian relations depend ultimately on American knowledge and understanding of Canada. We further believe that Canada must recognize the enormous benefits to their society that are coupled to the economic and cultural dominance of their giant neighbor. Furthermore, there is a need for both countries to understand their similarities in a dangerously divided world. If the Canadians find aspects of the U.S. world role distasteful, they would benefit from the realization that they, more than other nations, can influence that role.

It remains true, however, that the greatest knowledge gap exists in the United States; and the magnitude of the U.S.-Canadian relationship must be better understood there in order to receive the commitment it so badly needs. Furthermore, while few presidents have failed to publicly note the importance of the relationship, the fact remains that the conduct of U.S.-Canadian relations, albeit unintentionally, slips into a low priority status when competing with countless international and domestic crises demanding presidential attention. Any number of new international commissions, committees, and additional high-level personnel could not be successful in improving the relationship without a clear policy direction from the president.

This concluding chapter presents the authors' recommendations in the form of a prescription for future action that is offered as an example of what can and must be considered. First and foremost, the president must assign a high priority to U.S.-Canadian relations if an adequate governmental response is to be expected.

A New Canada Policy

As a first step we recommend that the president call for the development in Washington of a "New Canada Policy," which would be designed to avoid future ruptures, maintain good relations, and keep options open for future desirable collaboration.

The implementation of the New Canada Policy would encompass some immediate institutional changes to enhance the management of the intensive day-to-day activities of the relationship, improve the treaty-making process, and deal with the complex and often rupturable bilateral economic problems. Our government seemingly does not recognize that the magnitude and nature of the U.S.-Canadian relationship requires a special handling beyond traditional norms. The pace of activity and disbursement of U.S. government responsibilities leaves Canada in an odd position, as if it were the fifty-first state or alternately an unfamiliar nation with whom relations must proceed through strict diplomatic channels. In short, the diplomatic and bureaucratic machinery in Washington is not geared to meet the current demands.

The State Department assigns to an assistant secretary of state and a single deputy the direct responsibility for European and Canadian affairs. This arrangement spreads the leadership responsibility too thin for both areas. We recommend that the position of Deputy Assistant Secretary of State for Canadian Affairs be created. The deputy assistant secretary should be given the staff and the clear authority to oversee the management of U.S.-Canadian bilateral problems within all departments and agencies of the federal government, thus bringing greater coherence to the current fragmentation of that effort. The deputy assistant secretary should be encouraged to become a familiar figure on Capitol Hill in order that members of Congress would have ready access to current U.S. policy information. Such access would enhance U.S. ability to resolve differences of current concern to both countries.

There has been an historic concern that to provide a special structure for the conduct of foreign policy with Canada and Mexico would cause similar expectations in other important nations, or would somehow unbalance the equality of treatment given to other countries of importance to U.S. interests. However, one could easily argue that by sharing this continent with Canada and Mexico, our mutual problems and opportunities are unique. Accordingly, it would not seem indefensible to name an Assistant Secretary of State for Canadian Affairs, as well as perhaps an Assistant Secretary of State for Mexican Affairs. If this course were not implemented, we would then recommend that a lower ranking official be appointed to carry out a similar function.

A New Canada Policy would also envision the creation of formal and informal institutions. These would be designed not only to ease the solution of current problems but to identify and seek to avoid the problems whenever possible.

Treaty making between the two countries provides one such opportunity. The negotiation of any treaty itself is sufficient evidence of the existence of a matter of important bilateral concern, certain to be highly visible to the interested citizens of both countries. Government officials in both Canada and the United States are clearly aware of the constitutional differences in the ratification process. The prime minister's signature commits the Canadian government to a treaty's terms, while the president's approval requires ratification by a two-thirds vote in the United States Senate. In the case of the recent East Coast Fisheries Treaties, this was a requirement largely unknown to or unrealized by Canadian citizens. The fact that both treaties were approved by the president and the prime minister, only to become stalled in the United States Senate, left an impression that the United States had failed to live up to an important agreement. While this was not the case, serious damage to the bilateral relationship had needlessly occurred.

The constitutional separation of the legislative and executive branches of government is fundamental to the U.S. system and is an important distinction between our two forms of government. However, in many instances, Senate involvement early in the negotiation process would seem advisable. We recommend the establishment of an informal mechanism whereby representatives of the United States Senate could either participate in the negotiation of treaties or, preferably, serve in a formal advisory capacity to the president and his negotiating team. Presidential appointment of Senate representatives would be consistent with their constitutional duty to "advise and consent," would leave treaty initiatives clearly with the Executive, and perhaps would avoid the embarrassment of making a commitment to Canada that could not be upheld.

Further in the legislative arena, we recommend the establishment of a permanent structure, perhaps a Subcommittee on U.S.-Canadian Relations, under the aegis of the House Foreign Affairs Committee, to deal strictly with all aspects of U.S.-Canadian relations. Such a subcommittee would provide a much-needed focus for informing Congress of the bilateral implications of its actions—so many of which actions, though usually unintentionally, are of great consequence to Canada.

The Commission Concept

It remains, however, that most of the bilateral problems between the United States and Canada are rooted in economic concerns. Here again, we find a vital need for a coordination of policy and effort within the U.S. bureaucracy. Trade issues frequently ricochet between the Treasury Department, the International Trade Division of the Department of Commerce, the president's Special Trade Representative, or the office of the Assistant Secretary of State for Economic and Business Affairs. There should be a clearly assigned oversight function vested in the State Department. A potential two-way trade that can easily exceed $100 billion per year demands more concise management than the current ad hoc arrangement. The creation of a bilateral economic commission or series of commissions fashioned after the successful International Joint Commission is a proposal that has frequently surfaced. With representatives from both countries backed by a technical staff, the commission would recommend solutions to current economic problems to both governments for their action.

The commission concept would have the advantage of providing a readily identifiable and skilled mechanism free from special interest pressures to negotiate balanced solutions to economic disputes with long-term economic health as its criteria.

Single-issue economic commissions have been proposed to deal with such important but troublesome concerns as fisheries rights and the Auto Pact. Some special binational committees modeled after the IJC have been established, such as the Permanent Joint Board of Defense or the Joint Ministerial Committee on Trade and Economic Affairs. The Permanent Joint Board of Defense still functions, but largely in an advisory capacity. Although the Joint Ministerial Committee on Trade and Economic Affairs no longer exists, its reemergence is often suggested, but relegated to an informal structure.

Because there is a strong linkage between economic problems and private sector interest groups, the negotiation of those problems often involves national policy. Hence, the ad hoc approach to economic problem solving prevails. It is precisely because our economic interdependence is so vital to the welfare of both countries, so potentially disruptive to the relationship, and so tied to future opportunities that *we believe the uncoordinated ad hoc approach should be replaced.* The order and formalization associated with commissions is a necessary part of that replacement.

Our Recommendation

Having rejected the current uncoordinated approach that is no longer capable of maintaining the relationship in a healthy and productive state, it is incumbent upon us to recommend a replacement program. Valuing stability and predictability over instability and uncertainty, and being willing to trade some of the present flexibility of "ad hockery" for the values of stability that other approaches offer, we recommend that the following two precepts be adopted:

That the new program of conduct in U.S.-Canadian relations be formal and institutional in nature; that it be governed by clear rules of procedure; that these rules be incorporated ultimately into a new set of agreements and treaties, and that Washington's New Canada Policy clearly call for such; and that, granted the uniqueness and enormity of the scope of the U.S.-Canadian nongovernmental or private sector relationship, that sufficient and diverse representation of the private sector be encouraged in every way possible, such representation to include, but not be limited to, leaders of business and industry, finance, labor, citizens' organizations, and academia, provided that such private citizens have clear expertise in U.S.-Canadian relations (and, in the case of Americans, clear knowledge of Canada and matters Canadian); and

That encouragement and support be given to subnational government, and particularly to U.S. state governments, to develop Canadian expertise so that matters more properly in the domain of state and provincial government can be managed and differences resolved at that level, and so that the future relationship can be strengthened at something more akin to a grass-roots level.

These precepts are designed for adoption by both peoples, but it is clear that since the need is greatest south of the border, their applicability is also greatest south of the border. It is the American people who are most able to bring about any fundamental change in the relationship. It is they, with their ten-fold greater numbers and their vast economic and political power, who hold most of the cards.

How might these precepts be implemented?

In the bilateral arena, the two precepts might well be implemented simultaneously, through the establishment of a series of needed commissions patterned somewhat on the IJC model. Because this must be a long-term objective, we recommend the establishment of a U.S.-Canadian *Joint Economic Commission,* with adequate staff empowered to draw upon the expertise of technical personnel within the specialized departments of both governments. The U.S.-Canadian Joint Economic Commission would be charged with the responsibility of maintaining a current perspective on all aspects of the economic relationship, predicting future problem areas, and making balanced action recommendations to both governments.

Such a Joint Economic Commission should contain within its membership a private sector financier, a senior executive of an industry with strong U.S.-Canadian trade links, a labor leader of an international union, and a citizen group leader, perhaps representing consumer interests—as well as appropriate federal officials from the diplomatic and economic bureaucracies. There might, of course, be a fear of conflict of interest with some private sector representatives; but the values to be gained by appointing people with long commitments and vital interests in the bilateral economic area should outweigh any conflict-of-interest disadvantages. Private sector representatives would abstain from commission activity directly involving their own organization or its interests. The IJC model of terms for the commissioners, mandatory semi-annual meetings alternating between the two countries, organization of small permanent technical staffs, and appointments of specialized boards and committees to tackle specific problems could well form the organizational base of such a commission. The commission's output would be in the form of public but nonbinding recommendations to government and, unlike the IJC at present, the commission would (and should) have the power to initiate its activities within some broad prescribed guidelines.

As the ultimate solution and as a matter of policy, we recommend that both countries continue to move slowly and deliberately toward bilateral free trade. However, the transition should be projected over an extended period of time and move at a pace that provides a clear window of mutual benefit, a balanced fair treatment, and minimal disruption to established business.

In light of the four disputed maritime boundaries, allied fishery and energy disputes, and differences in the Arctic over matters of sovereignty and pollution, we recommend the establishment of a *Sea and Shore Boundaries and Resources Commission* to carry out for the marine environment what the IJC has done for the inland freshwater environment, as well as to insure the fair adjudication of the four boundary sovereignty disputes. Such a commission should contain representation from the fishery and energy industries, one or more academic scientists from an appropriate marine science discipline, and representatives from a sample of coastal states and provinces. The U.S. staff might well be headquartered in the Pacific Northwest or New England, the Canadian staff on the opposite coast in the Maritimes or British Columbia, to give the states, provinces, and affected interests greater access and to decentralize the role of the national capitals. Otherwise, this commission could likewise derive value from the IJC model.

Both nations have benefited from the superb example of IJC joint data gathering and monitoring, as well as the research skills of the IJC staff. This experience teaches us that there is much benefit to be gained by furthering the cause of U.S.-Canadian research endeavors in a host of scientific and technical fields. Such research should not be conducted merely for dispute avoidance but rather for the value of working together to solve common problems and to contribute to world peace. Medicine, environmental science, energy technology, agricultural and forestry research, space research, and research in the pure sciences and in countless other fields could well be coordinated by both governments for mutual and perhaps even for global benefit. Beyond needed government contributions earmarked for such joint research is the need for a bilateral Joint Research Commission, composed of government, industry, and academic scientists from all major pure and applied disciplines that could coordinate and conduct research in both countries, and organize programs whereby scientists and engineers in each country could work in the other country as easily as in their own. Initial research thrusts might focus on those problems that divide or threaten to divide the two peoples (with government commitment to accept the findings of such joint research as their own), but later endeavors could focus much more broadly on those areas that promise mutual benefit.

Finally, the *International Joint Commission,* in many ways an excellent model, should be greatly strengthened. A broad review of its activities is called for to determine why it has not received stronger support and how this problem might be remedied. A campaign to publicize the IJC and make it better known, particularly to the American people, is very much in order. A clear constituency for the commission must be identified and its awareness elevated. While in truth the IJC's constituency is everyone with a stake in healthy U.S.-Canadian relations—in other words, every citizen in both countries—residents of border communities and the Great Lakes Basin, certain states and provinces, and certain industries have a more direct stake. The awareness level of these constituencies must be elevated. Finally, while membership on the commission could remain the current small number (six), efforts should be made to more formally facilitate the input of the many industries, labor unions, states, provinces, Great Lakes users, local governments, and citizen groups who are affected by the decisions and recommendations of the commission. This goal might be accomplished through the establishment of an advisory committee to the commission, composed of representatives of those involved interests, that met with the commission on a regular basis. The International Joint Commission is not so much in need of radical overhaul as it is in need of substantially greater recognition of what it can accomplish and the wherewithal to do the job, as an independent vehicle of both governments under the Boundary Waters Treaty.

The third concept, that of encouraging and strengthening the states (and to a lesser extent the already very capable provinces), is very much in keeping with the forces of decentralization now at work in both nations. In serving their own direct interests, the states can serve their nation's interests, as well as the cause of continental relations. The most active states in this regard are those along the Canadian border, the residents of which must live amicably with their Canadian neighbors. They are the people who have the most to gain from healthy relations and the most to lose from unhealthy relations. Given this incentive and given the insight that comes from living in the affected region, state governments are in a good position to carry on their shoulders a much greater proportion of the bilateral relations burden. We recommend that the federal government encourage greater activity (through the National Governors Association or some similar vehicle) and involvement in the type of informal interchanges that have been occurring on a selective basis so successfully between some of the states and provinces.

While the management of U.S.-Canadian relations is by necessity a governmental responsibility, good relations can be enhanced by nongovernmental activities. For example, the continued expansion of U.S.-Canadian studies programs in our universities is an excellent vehicle for the involvement of the academic community in long-term growth of awareness. The U.S. government should consider supplementing the efforts of the Canadian government and the private Donner Foundation by supporting these programs and insuring their viability.

A concerted effort on the part of the U.S. news media to increase Canadian coverage in the United States would contribute in the short term to a greater consciousness and to our ability to share the North American continent. The present two-tenths of one percent of coverage devoted to Canada is insufficient.

In other words, the people of both nations must be made more aware. Encouragement of increased media attention can help us to achieve this goal in the short term, while support for formal education can help to achieve it in the longer term.

Are Canada and the United States Up to the Challenge?

As has been stated many times in this book, the knowledge of the American people about Canada is woefully inadequate, perhaps dangerously so. And, as these two nations diverge in their views of the world and in their foreign policies, a new and perhaps even more dangerous dimension of this inadequacy is arising: Americans must recognize and accept Canada's perception of its global role. (The Canadian people's knowledge of U.S. foreign policy, and the motives behind it, is perhaps as great as the average American's knowledge of his own nation's foreign policy, so the ignorance referred to is clearly one-sided.)

Canada is clearly not the fifty-first American state. Nor is Canada an ally that follows Washington's lead mindlessly and commits to American positions automatically. Canada is dominated by the United States only to the extent it must be (mainly economically, and less so with time) to avoid traumatic harm to its economy and society. Its worldview is seemingly different and increasingly differing from that of the United States. And yet, Canada represents opportunity for the United States, culturally, economically, socially, politically. This opportunity can be decreased or lost through choice, with full knowledge of the alternatives, or through default, by failing to pay them heed. To give our bilateral relationship some insurance against those difficulties and differences, those stresses and strains that are inevitable, it behooves the governments and peoples of both countries to begin now to build up a reservoir of good will in all possible ways, a reservoir that can be drawn upon as need arises. Such insurance can provide dividends well beyond the cost of the investment.

Bibliography

Beigie, Carl and Hero, Alfred O., Jr. *Natural Resources in U.S.-Canadian Relations.* Vols. 1 and 2, Boulder Colorado: Westview Press, 1980.

Brebner, J. Bartlett. *Canada: A Modern History.* Ann Arbor: University of Michigan Press, 1960.

Carroll, John E. and Logan, Rod. *The Garrison Diversion Issue: A Case Study in U.S.-Canadian Environmental Relations.* Montreal: Canada-U.S. Future Prospects Series, C.D. Howe Institute, 1980.

Carroll, John E. *Acid Rain: An Issue in Canadian-American Relations.* Washington and Toronto: Canadian-American Committee, 1982.

Carroll, John E. *Environmental Diplomacy: An Examination and Prospective of Canadian-U.S. Transboundary Environmental Relations.* Ann Arbor: University of Michigan Press, 1983.

Clarkson, Stephen. *Canada and the Reagan Challenge.* Toronto: James Lorimer & Co., Publishers, in association with the Canadian Institute for Economic Policy, 1982.

Dickey, John Sloan. *Canada and the American Presence: The United States Interest in an Independent Canada.* New York: New York University Press, 1975.

Hero, Alfred O. and Daneau, Marcel. *Problems and Opportunities in U.S.-Quebec Relations.* Boulder, Colorado: Westview Press, 1983.

Holmes, John W. *Life With Uncle: The Canadian-American Relationship.* Toronto: University of Toronto Press, 1981.

Spencer, Robert, et al., eds, *The International Joint Commission Seventy Years On.* Toronto: University of Toronto Centre for International Studies, 1981.

Swanson, Roger Frank. *Intergovernmental Perspectives on the Canada-U.S. Relationship.* New York: New York University Press, 1978.

Willoughby, William R. *The Joint Organizations of Canada and the United States.* Toronto: University of Toronto Press, 1979.

Index

About the Authors

Kenneth M. Curtis is a lawyer and political leader with considerable involvement in Canadian affairs. He has served as a congressional aide, secretary of state for Maine, governor of Maine for eight years, chairman of the New England Governors Conference, and chairman of the Democratic National Committee.

While governor, Mr. Curtis was instrumental in forming the New England Governors and Eastern Canadian Premiers Conference, active in relations with the provinces of New Brunswick, Nova Scotia and Quebec. More recently, he served as a member of the United States/Canadian International Joint Commission (1978-1979), and United States Ambassador to Canada (1979-1981).

John E. Carroll is an associate professor of environmental conservation at the University of New Hampshire and is a Kellogg Foundation National Fellow in international environmental relations. An internationally known specialist in Canadian-U.S. environmental and energy relations, he is the author of *Environmental Diplomacy: An Examination and Prospective of Canadian-U.S. Transboundary Environmental Relations* (1983), and *Acid Rain: An Issue in Canadian-American Relations* (1982), and is coauthor of *The Garrison Diversion Unit: A Case Study in Canadian-U.S. Environmental Relations* (1980). He has also written numerous articles and organized conferences on various aspects of the bilateral environmental relationship. He has been visiting professor at Vermont Law School lecturing on Canadian-American environmental diplomacy, and has been recognized for his scholarship by membership in Phi Kappa Phi.